iPad® with iOS 11 for Seniors

Seekonk Public Library
410 Newman Ave.
Seekonk, MA 02771

3 1658 00372 7219

Studio Visual Steps

iPad® with iOS 11 for Seniors

Learn to work with the iPad with iOS 11

www.visualsteps.com

This book has been written using the Visual Steps™ method.
Cover design by Studio Willemien Haagsma bNO

© 2017 Visual Steps
Author: Studio Visual Steps

First printing: October 2017
ISBN 978 90 5905 424 0

All rights reserved. No part of this publication may be reproduced, stored in a retrieval system or transmitted in any form or by any means, electronic, mechanical, photocopying, recording, scanning or otherwise, except as permitted under Sections 107 or 108 of the 1976 United States Copyright Act, without the prior written permission of the Publisher.

LIMIT OF LIABILITY/DISCLAIMER OF WARRANTY: While the publisher and author have used their best efforts in preparing this book, they make no representations or warranties with respect to the accuracy or completeness of the contents of this book and specifically disclaim any implied warranties of merchantability or fitness for a particular purpose. No warranty may be created or extended by sales representatives or written sales materials. The advice and strategies contained herein may not be suitable for your situation. You should consult with a professional where appropriate. Neither the publisher nor author shall be liable for any loss of profit or any other commercial damages, including but not limited to special, incidental, consequential or other damages.

Trademarks: This book contains names of registered trademarks. iPad is a registered trademark of Apple, Inc. All other trademarks are the property of their respective owners. Visual Steps Publishing is not associated with any product or vendor mentioned in this book.
In the text of this book, these names are not indicated by their trademark symbol, because they are solely used for identifying the products which are mentioned in the text. In no way does this constitute an infringement on the rights of the trademark owners.

Resources used: A number of definitions and explanations of computer terminology are taken over from the *iPad User Guide*.

Do you have questions or suggestions?
Email: info@visualsteps.com

Would you like more information?
www.visualsteps.com

Website for this book:
www.visualsteps.com/ipad11

Subscribe to the free Visual Steps Newsletter:
www.visualsteps.com/newsletter

Table of Contents

Foreword

The iPad is an extremely user-friendly, portable multimedia device with countless possibilities. This device is ideal for all sorts of purposes, for instance surfing the Internet, sending and receiving emails, taking notes, or keeping a diary.

But this useful device has much more to offer. There are a number of standard apps (programs) available for working with photos, video, and music. You can even look up addresses and well-known places around the world, with *Maps*.
Also, you can go to the *App Store* and download numerous free and paid apps and games. What about recipes, horoscopes, fitness exercises, and stories to read aloud? You name it, and there will be some useful app to be got.

In this book you will get acquainted with the main functions and options of the iPad, step by step and at your own pace.

You can work through this useful book independently. Put the book next to your iPad and execute all the operations, step by step. The clear instructions and multitude of screen shots will tell you exactly what to do.
This is the quickest way of learning to use the iPad. Simply by doing it. A whole new world will appear!

We wish you lots of fun in working with the iPad!

Studio Visual Steps

PS After you have worked through this book, you will know how to send an email. We welcome your comments and suggestions. Our email address is: info@visualsteps.com

Visual Steps Newsletter

All Visual Steps books follow the same methodology: clear and concise step-by-step instructions with screen shots to demonstrate each task. A complete list of all our books can be found on our website **www.visualsteps.com** You can also sign up to receive our **free Visual Steps Newsletter**.
In this Newsletter you will receive periodic information by email regarding:
- the latest titles and previously released books;
- special offers, supplemental chapters, tips and free informative booklets.
Also, our Newsletter subscribers may download any of the documents listed on the web pages **www.visualsteps.com/info_downloads**

When you subscribe to our Newsletter you can be assured that we will never use your email address for any purpose other than sending you the information as previously described. We will not share this address with any third-party. Each Newsletter also contains a one-click link to unsubscribe.

Introduction to Visual Steps™

The Visual Steps handbooks and manuals are the best instructional materials available for learning how to work with the iPad and other computers. Nowhere else can you find better support for getting to know an iPad, the Internet, *Windows*, *MacOS*, a Samsung Galaxy Tab and computer programs.

Properties of the Visual Steps books:
- **Comprehensible contents**
  Addresses the needs of the beginner or intermediate computer user for a manual written in simple, straight-forward English.
- **Clear structure**
  Precise, easy to follow instructions. The material is broken down into small enough segments to allow for easy absorption.
- **Screen shots of every step**
  Quickly compare what you see on your screen with the screen shots in the book. Pointers and tips guide you when new windows are opened so you always know what to do next.
- **Get started right away**
  All you have to do is turn on your device, place the book next to it and execute the operations on your own iPad.
- **Layout**
  The text is printed in a large size font. Even if you put the book next to your iPad, this font will be clearly legible.

In short, I believe these manuals will be excellent guides for you.

dr. H. van der Meij
Faculty of Applied Education, Department of Instruction Technology, University of Twente, the Netherlands

What You Will Need

To be able to work through this book, you will need a number of things:

Suitable for all iPads with *iOS 11* or higher.

For more information, see the webpage
www.visualsteps.com/ipad11

A computer or a notebook computer with the *iTunes* program installed. In *Appendix B Installing iTunes and Connecting the iPad to the Computer* you can read how to install *iTunes* and set it up for use with your iPad.

If you do not own a computer or notebook, you may be able to execute these operations on the computer of a friend or family member. It is not necessary to have a computer while working with an iPad.

How to Use This Book

This book has been written using the Visual Steps™ method. The method is simple: you put the book next to your iPad and execute all the tasks step by step, directly on your iPad. Because of the clear instructions and the multitude of screen shots, you will know exactly what to do. By executing all the tasks at once, you will learn how to use the iPad in the quickest possible way.
In this Visual Steps™ book, you will see various icons. This is what they mean:

Techniques
These icons indicate an action to be carried out:

The index finger indicates you need to do something on the iPad's screen, for instance, tap something.

The keyboard icon means you should type something on the keyboard of your iPad or your computer.

The mouse icon means you should do something on your computer with the mouse.

The hand icon means you should do something else, for example rotate the iPad or switch it off. The hand will also be used for a series of operations which you have learned at an earlier stage.

Apart from these operations, in some parts of this book extra assistance is provided to help you successfully work through this book.

Help
These icons indicate that extra help is available:

 The arrow icon warns you about something.

  The bandage icon will help you if something has gone wrong.

Have you forgotten how to do something? The number next to the footsteps tells you where to look it up at the end of the book in the appendix *How Do I Do That Again?*

In separate boxes you will find general information or tips concerning the iPad.

Extra information
Information boxes are denoted by these icons:

 The book icon gives you extra background information that you can read at your convenience. This extra information is not necessary for working through the book.

 The light bulb icon indicates an extra tip for using the iPad.

Website

On the website that accompanies this book, **www.visualsteps.com/ipad11**, you will find more information about this book. This website will also keep you informed of changes you need to know as a user of the book. Visit this website regularly and check if there are any recent updates or additions to this book, or possible errata.

Test Your Knowledge

After you have worked through this book, you can test your knowledge online, at the **www.ccforseniors.com** website. By answering a number of multiple choice questions you will be able to test your knowledge of the iPad.
After you have finished the test, you will receive a *Computer Certificate*. Participating in the test is **free of charge**. The computer certificate website is a free Visual Steps service.

For Teachers

The Visual Steps books have been written as self-study guides for individual use. Although these books are also well suited for use in a group or a classroom setting. For this purpose, some of our books come with a free teacher's manual. You can download the available teacher's manuals and additional materials at:
www.visualsteps.com/instructor
After you have registered at this website, you can use this service for free.

The Screen Shots

The screen shots in this book indicate which button, file or hyperlink you need to tap on your iPad screen or click on your computer. In the instruction text (in **bold** letters) you will see a small image of the item you need to tap or click. The line will point you to the right place on your screen.
The small screen shots that are printed in this book are not meant to be completely legible all the time. This is not necessary, as you will see these images on your own iPad screen in real size and fully legible.

Here you see an example of such an instruction text and a screen shot of the item you need to tap. The line indicates where to find this item on your own screen:

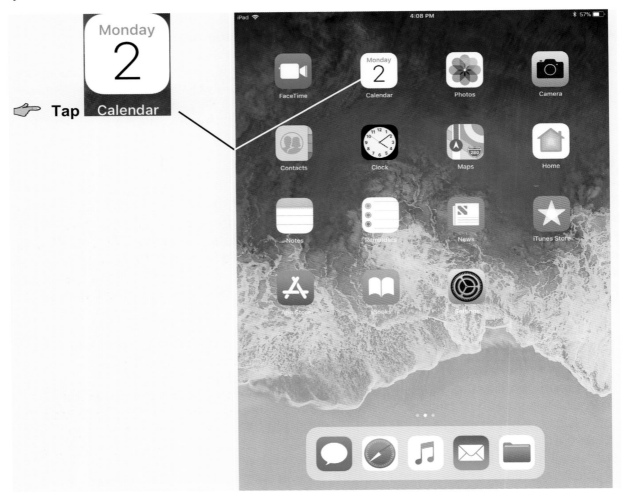

In some cases, the screen shot only displays part of the screen. Below you see an example of this:

At the bottom of the screen:

We would like to emphasize that we **do not intend you** to read the information in all of the screen shots in this book. Always use the screen shots in combination with the display on your iPad screen.

1. The iPad

Since the introduction of the first iPad in January 2010, millions of iPads have been sold. The iPad has now become one of the best selling tablet computers in the world. There are several editions of the iPad available today, but each iPad works in the same way.

The popularity of the iPad is not so surprising if you consider how lightweight and portable the iPad is and how easy it is to use. It has many of the same functions and capabilities of a regular computer. Not only can you surf the Internet and send and receive emails, you can also maintain a calendar, play games or read your favorite book, newspaper or magazine. You can also take pictures or make a movie and view or share them easily with others. You can do all this by using the so-called *apps*, the programs that are installed on the iPad. Along with the standard apps supplied on your iPad, you can easily add more (free and paid) by visiting the *App Store*, the web shop with all the apps.

In this chapter you will get to know your iPad. Depending on the type you have purchased, you connect to the Internet through a wireless network (Wi-Fi), or through the mobile data network with 3G or 4G, and look for updates.
You will also look at the *Notification Center*. Here you can view and manage the notifications on your iPad, such as new email messages, and any notifications you may have set for your calendar. Furthermore, you are going to look at the Dock, from where you can open apps, and the *Control Center*, where you will find several buttons for frequently used functions.

In this chapter you will learn about:

- turning the iPad on or waking it up from sleep mode;
- initial setup;
- the most important components of your iPad;
- updating the iPad;
- some basic operations for the iPad;
- connecting to the Internet via a wireless network (Wi-Fi);
- connecting to the Internet via the mobile data network;
- putting the iPad into sleep mode or turning it off.

 Please note:

You might see different screens during the setup of your iPad. This depends on the type of iPad you are using. In that case, follow the onscreen instructions.

1.1 Turning the iPad On or Waking it Up From Sleep Mode

The iPad can be turned off or locked. If your iPad is turned off, here is how you turn it on:

☞ **Press and hold the Sleep/Wake button until you see the Apple logo**

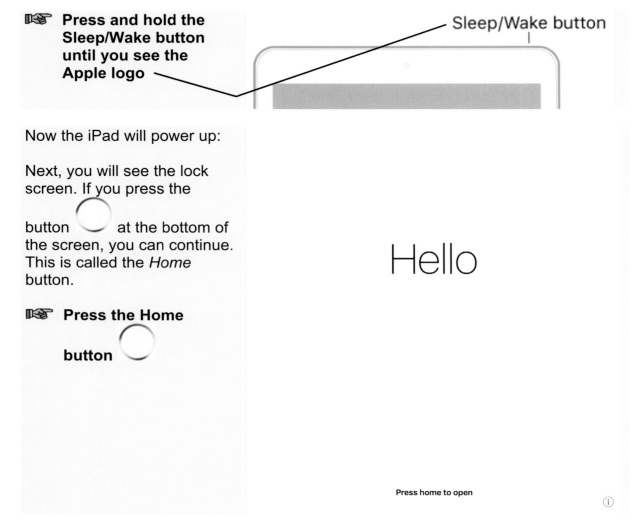

Now the iPad will power up:

Next, you will see the lock screen. If you press the button at the bottom of the screen, you can continue. This is called the *Home* button.

☞ **Press the Home button**

Hello

Press home to open

The iPad may also be locked. This is called *sleep mode*. If your iPad is locked, you can unlock it in the following way:

☞ **Press the Home button**

1.2 Initial Set Up of the iPad

When you start up your iPad for the very first time you will see a few screens where you are asked to enter some basic information. If you have already used your iPad before, you can skip this section and go to page 24.

Most operations on the iPad can be executed by tapping the screen. You tap the screen with one finger, for example, you index finger. Just follow the operations in this book, then you will see how this works.

You will set up the language:

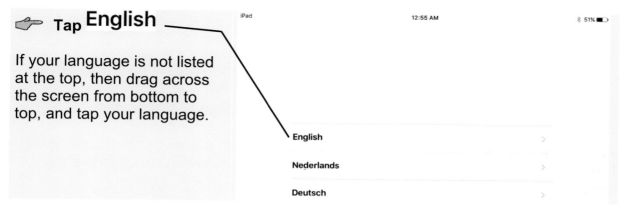

☞ **Tap English**

If your language is not listed at the top, then drag across the screen from bottom to top, and tap your language.

The next screen appears. Here you will select your country:

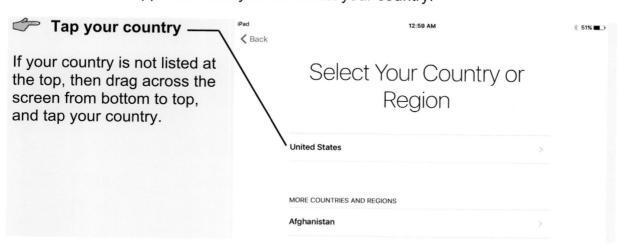

☞ **Tap your country**

If your country is not listed at the top, then drag across the screen from bottom to top, and tap your country.

You may see a screen regarding the automatic setup of the iPad. In this example you will skip this option:

 ☞ **Tap *Set Up Manually***

In the next screen, you will be asked to choose your Wi-Fi network to connect to the Internet:

 Tap your network

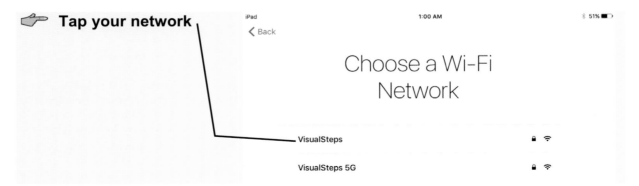

iPad   1:00 AM   ☀ 51% ■▢

‹ Back

Choose a Wi-Fi
Network

VisualSteps   🔒 📶

VisualSteps 5G   🔒 📶

🩹 Help! I don't have Wi-Fi.

You can only set up the iPad if you have a Wi-Fi network. There is an option for connecting your iPad to the Internet through the computer, with **Connect to iTunes**, but his method is very tedious.

If you have inserted a SIM card into your iPad in order to connect to the mobile data network, you will also see *Use Mobile Connection*, and then you can also use the SIM card to connect to the Internet.

Most Wi-Fi networks require you to enter a password, in order to establish a connection. You can do this by tapping the characters on the keyboard you see at the bottom of your screen. Later on in this book, we will explain in detail how to work with this onscreen keyboard.

⌨ **Type the password**

Does your password contain capital letters or numbers? Go to page 55 and 56 to read how to type them.

 **Tap Join**

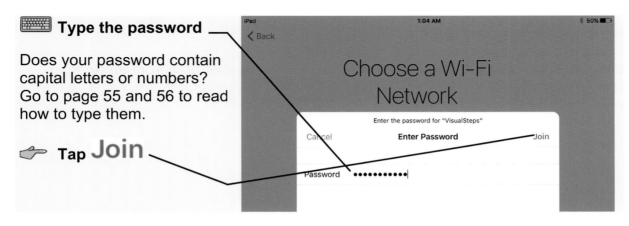

iPad   1:04 AM   ☀ 50% ■▢

‹ Back

Choose a Wi-Fi
Network

Enter the password for "VisualSteps"

Cancel   **Enter Password**   Join

Password   •••••••••|

The system tries to establish a connection. If this is successful:

☞ **Tap Next**

If you are using an iPad with 3G/4G, you may see an additional screen concerning the placement of your SIM card and checking the provider's settings. In *section 1.7 Connecting to the Internet Through the Mobile Data Network* you can read more about inserting a SIM card and connecting through the mobile data network.

 If necessary, tap Next or follow the instructions in the windows

On the latest type of iPads you will see an option to use your fingerprint (Touch ID) in place of a passcode. This is a security measure that can prevent others from using your iPad without you knowing it. In this example we will not yet set the Touch ID. You can do this later on, if you wish. This feature is explained in *Chapter 7 Changing Settings*. You are going to skip this step:

 Tap Set Up Touch ID Later

 Tap Don't use

You can also enter a passcode to unlock your iPad, if this has reverted to sleep mode, or has just been turned on. Just like Touch ID, this is a security measure that can prevent others from using your iPad without you noticing. The passcode consists of numbers.

In this example we will set a passcode. If you do not want this, you tap Passcode Options and then Don't Add Passcode.

⌨ **Type the desired passcode**

You will need to enter the code once more:

⌨ **Type the desired passcode again**

If you have already used an iPad before, or want to transfer data from an *Android* tablet or cell phone, the iPad has options for this. In this example, the iPad is configured as a new iPad:

👉 **If necessary, tap Set Up as New iPad**

Apps & Data

Restore from iCloud Backup   >

Restore from iTunes Backup   >

Set Up as New iPad   >

Move Data from Android   >

Please note:
You might see different screens during the setup of your iPad. This depends on the type of iPad you are using. In that case, follow the onscreen instructions.

You will be asked whether you want to sign in with an existing *Apple ID* or if you want to create a new one. An *Apple ID* consists of a combination of an email address and a password. You need to have an *Apple ID* to be able to download apps from the *App Store* and when using certain applications. If you already have an *Apple ID*:

☞ Tap next to Apple ID

⌨ Type your *Apple ID*

☞ Tap next to Password

⌨ Type your password

☞ Tap Next

☞ Continue on the next page, with the Terms and Conditions

If you do not yet have an *Apple ID*:

☞ Tap Don't have an Apple ID

☞ Tap Create a Free Apple ID

☞ Follow the onscreen instructions

In the next couple of screens you need to enter your data. You can use the keyboard for this, or you can select the desired options by tapping the screen.

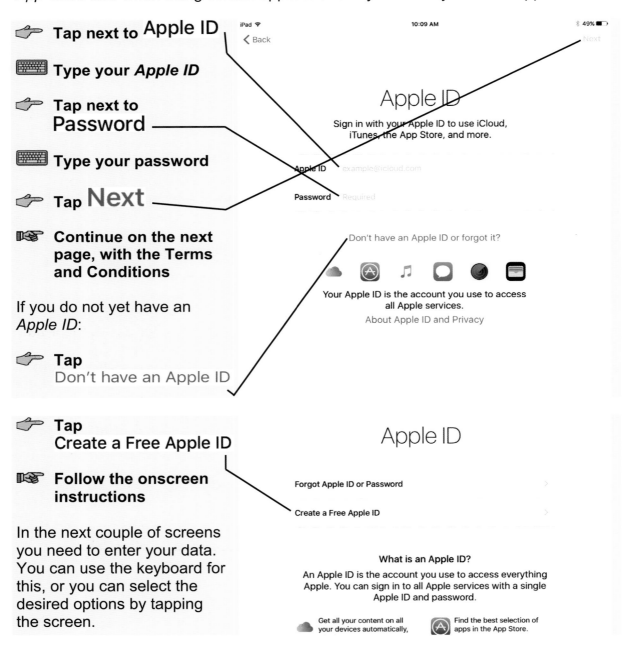

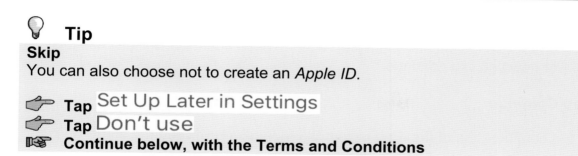

Tip

Skip

You can also choose not to create an *Apple ID*.

👉 **Tap** Set Up Later in Settings
👉 **Tap** Don't use
👉 **Continue below, with the Terms and Conditions**

The next screen displays Apple's Terms and Conditions. You must agree to these terms in order to be able to work with your iPad.

At the bottom of the screen:

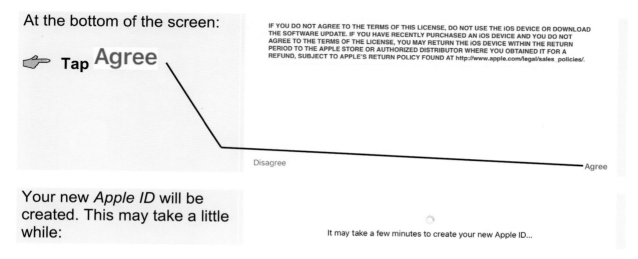

👉 **Tap Agree**

IF YOU DO NOT AGREE TO THE TERMS OF THIS LICENSE, DO NOT USE THE iOS DEVICE OR DOWNLOAD THE SOFTWARE UPDATE. IF YOU HAVE RECENTLY PURCHASED AN iOS DEVICE AND YOU DO NOT AGREE TO THE TERMS OF THE LICENSE, YOU MAY RETURN THE iOS DEVICE WITHIN THE RETURN PERIOD TO THE APPLE STORE OR AUTHORIZED DISTRIBUTOR WHERE YOU OBTAINED IT FOR A REFUND, SUBJECT TO APPLE'S RETURN POLICY FOUND AT http://www.apple.com/legal/sales_policies/.

Disagree   Agree

Your new *Apple ID* will be created. This may take a little while:

It may take a few minutes to create your new Apple ID...

You will see a screen concerning the so-called Express settings. Here you can agree to the use of *Siri*, and to sending data to Apple regarding your use of the iPad, for further analysis. With *Siri* you can give voice commands to the iPad. For example, you can ask for the weather forecast. In *section 4.7 Siri* you will find more information on *Siri*.
You are also warned that the *Location Services* option is enabled. With this option, the *Maps* app can collect and use data that approximately indicate your location, for instance. In this example, you will accept this option and continue. If you do not want to use these options, you tap *Customize Settings*.

👉 **Tap** *Continue*

You will see a similar window for analyzing the use of *iCloud*, a service provided by Apple, and for analyzing apps. Here you can choose not to share these data:

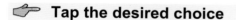

👉 **Tap the desired choice**

You may see a number of screens with information on new functions on the iPad, such as the Dock, and switching between recently used apps. We will discuss this later on. For now you just continue:

 **Tap** *Continue*

Finally, the configuration of the iPad is completed, and you will see the screen *Welcome to iPad*. Now you can get started:

☞ **Tap** Get Started

Now you will see the home screen with all the colored app icons:

Please note: the background of your iPad might be slightly different. This does not affect the steps you need to follow.

Help! My iPad is locked.

If you don't use your iPad for a little while, the home screen will lock itself. This happens after about two minutes of non-activity. You can unlock the iPad like this:

 Press the Home button

☞ **If necessary, enter the numbers of the passcode**

1.3 The Main Components of Your iPad

In the next images you will see the main components of the iPad. When we describe a certain operation in this book, you can look for the relevant component in these images.

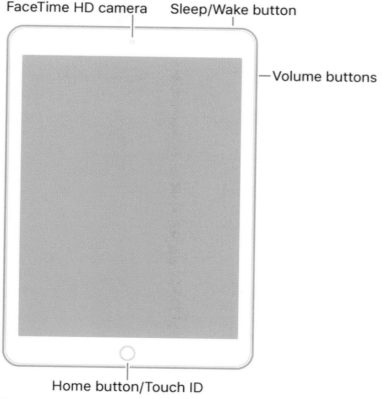

Source: User Guide iPad.

Seekonk Public Library

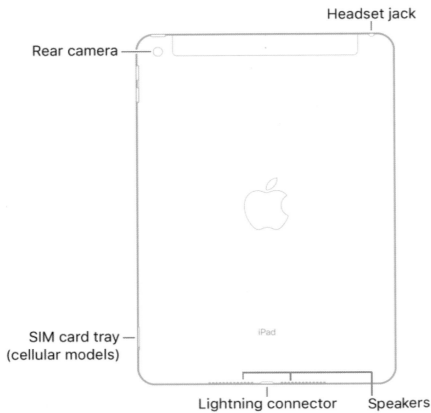

Source: User Guide iPad.

* The speakers of the iPad Pro are located at the upper edge of the iPad.
** On the iPad Pro a True Tone Flash is located under the rear camera.

On the status bar, located at the top of your iPad, various icons display information about the status of the iPad and its connections. Below you see an overview of all the most important status icons you might encounter along with their significance:

	This shows that the screen orientation is locked.
	The iPad is locked. This icon will be displayed when the lock screen appears.
	Battery is charging.
	Battery is fully charged.
	The iPad is connected to the computer, but the USB port does not provide enough power for charging the battery.
	Shows that a song, audio book or podcast is playing.

- Continue on the next page -

	Shows that the iPad has a Wi-Fi Internet connection. The more bars, the stronger the connection.
No SIM	No SIM card has been installed (in an iPad suited for Wi-Fi and 3G or 4G).
3G / **4G**	Shows that your carrier's mobile data network (iPad Wi-Fi + 3G or 4G) is available and you can connect to the Internet over 3G or 4G.
	Signal strength of the connection and name of the mobile network carrier currently in use.
E	Shows that your carrier's EDGE network (some iPad Wi-Fi + 3G or 4G models) is available and you can connect to the Internet with EDGE.
GPRS	Shows that your carrier's GPRS network (some iPad Wi-Fi + 3G or 4G models) is available and you can connect to the Internet with GPRS.
VPN	This icon appears when you are connected to a *Virtual Private Network* (VPN). VPNs are used in organizations, for secure sending of private information over a public network.
	This icon appears when a program uses location services. That means that information about your current location will be used.
	Shows network and other activity. Some apps may also use this symbol to indicate an active process.
	Bluetooth icon. If the icon is rendered in white, it means Bluetooth has been enabled, but no device is connected. If a device is connected, the icon will be displayed in another color.
	Airplane mode is on. If your iPad is in this mode, you do not have access to the Internet and you cannot use Bluetooth devices.

1.4 Updating the iPad

Apple is regularly issuing new updates for the iPad software, called *iOS*, and software for apps. In these updates, existing problems are fixed or new functions are added. Normally, these updates will be downloaded automatically to your iPad. But we would advise you to regularly check if there are any updates available for your iPad. If necessary, wake your iPad up from sleep:

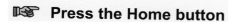 **Press the Home button**

☞ **If necessary, tap the numbers of the passcode**

Now you will see the home screen of your iPad. This is how to open the *Settings* app:

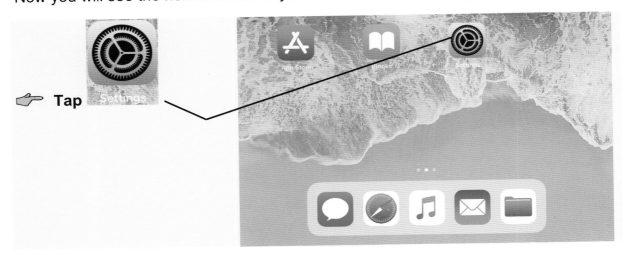

☞ **Tap** *Settings*

🐦 **Please note:**

In this book we always use the iPad in portrait mode, where the longer side is vertically positioned. We recommend using your iPad in portrait mode while you work through the chapters in this book, otherwise you may see a screen that is different from the examples shown.

Here you see the *Settings* app:

The *General* section is already opened: ―――――

☞ **Tap** Software Update

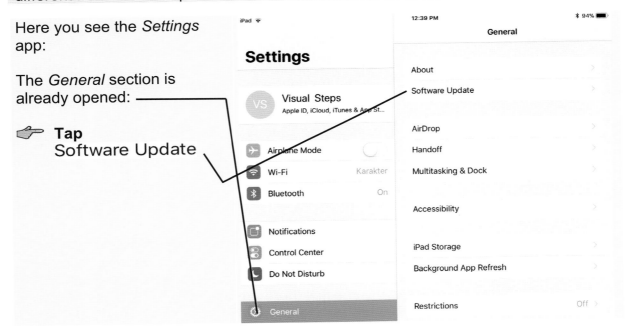

Now the iPad will check if there is any new software available.

In this example, the iPad
already has the current
software version installed:

To return to the *General*
section:

☞ **Tap** ❮ General

If a newer version is found, you will see a message about the update.

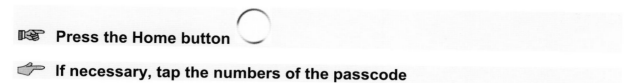

☞ **Follow the onscreen instructions**

When the update has been installed, you will return to the home screen. If you did
not go back to the home screen, you press the Home button:

☞ **Press the Home button** ◯

1.5 Some Basic iPad Operations

The iPad is easy to use. You will practice some basic operations and touch
movements. If necessary, wake your iPad up from sleep:

☞ **Press the Home button** ◯

☞ **If necessary, tap the numbers of the passcode**

You will see the home screen of the iPad. You will open *Settings* again:

☞ **Tap** Settings

If necessary, tap
General

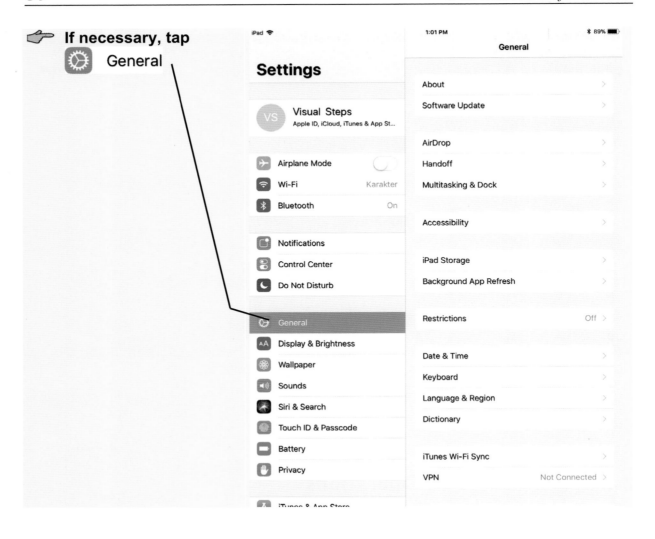

You have already used the tapping gesture a number of times. Another frequently used gesture is swiping. This too, is done with your index finger. When you do this, you make a swiping gesture across the screen:

☞ **Place your finger halfway on the right-hand side of the screen and drag upwards**

The right-hand side of the screen will move upwards, and you will see the elements at the bottom of the list:

You can drag downwards in the same way. You can also use this swiping gesture on the left-hand side of the screen.

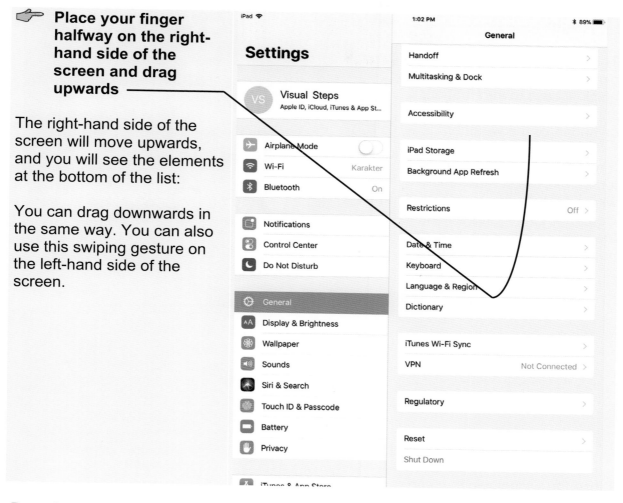

Dragging can also be done on the edges of the iPad. Just try it:

☞ **Drag downwards from the top of the screen**

The *Notification Center* is opened. Messages are displayed here as well. You will probably not see any messages yet, because you have not yet used any apps.

You can also open other screens from within the *Notification Center*:

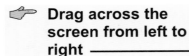 **Drag across the screen from left to right** ──────

The widget screen is displayed. Widgets provide quick access to information, such as an event list in the calendar, or the weather:

If now you drag from right to left across the screen, you will go back to the *Notification Center*. If you do this again, the camera will open. You do not need to do this right now.

Close the widget window and go back to the *Settings* app:

 **Press the Home button**

Dragging from the bottom of the screen opens an option too:

☞ **Drag across the screen from bottom to top** ———

You will see the Dock. This is a central place, where frequently used apps are displayed:

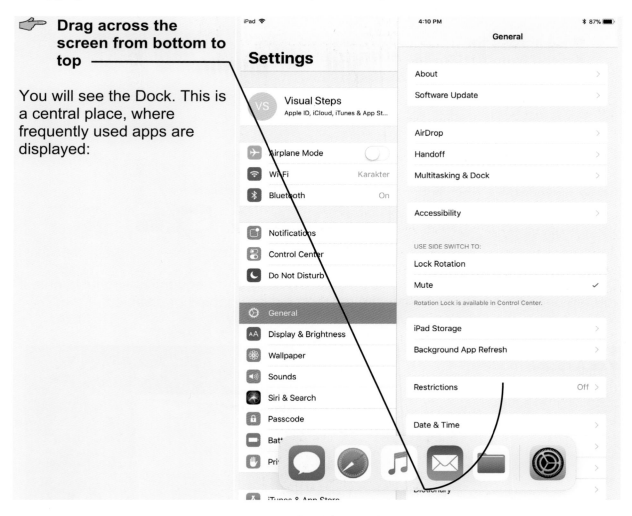

You will go back:

☞ **Press the Home button**

If an app is opened, in this case the *Settings* app you see on your screen right now, you can use the Home button to go back to the home screen on the iPad:

☞ **Press the Home button**

Dragging from the top of the home screen will open the *Notification Center* again. If you drag from the bottom of the home screen, the *Control Center* will open:

☞ **Drag across the screen from bottom to top**

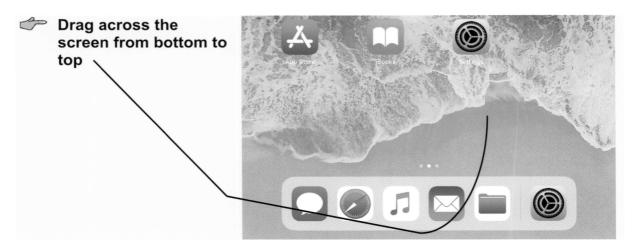

On the *Control Center*, you will see the opened apps and frequently used functions. If you tap one of the buttons below, the function will be enabled or disabled. If the button is blue, the function is enabled:

Airplane mode:

AirDrop:

Wi-Fi:

Bluetooth:

Controls of the *Music* app:

Set screen brightness by dragging:

Set volume by dragging:

Synchronize with another Apple device:

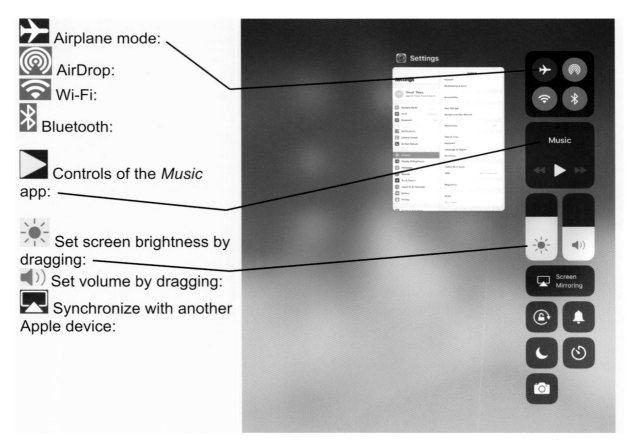

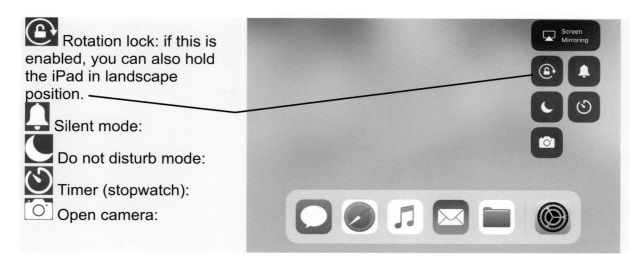

Rotation lock: if this is enabled, you can also hold the iPad in landscape position.

Silent mode:

Do not disturb mode:

Timer (stopwatch):

Open camera:

You will go back to the home screen:

☞ **Press the Home button**

By now you have practiced some basic operations and touch gestures. Of course there are even more touch gestures, such as scrolling, zooming in and out, and using the keyboard. These gestures will be discussed in the chapters where you will need to use them.

1.6 Connecting to the Internet Through Wi-Fi

You may have already connected to the Internet while you were setting up your iPad. But it can happen that the default network is not available. Perhaps you are using the iPad at a different location or your own default network is temporarily down for some reason. If you have access to a wireless network, you can connect to the Internet with that.

Now, go back to the *Settings* app you used in previous steps:

☞ **Open the *Settings* app** ✌[1]

To connect to a Wi-Fi network:

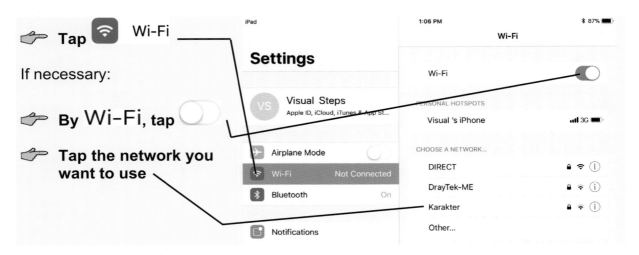

☞ **Tap** 🛜 **Wi-Fi**

If necessary:

☞ **By Wi-Fi, tap**

☞ **Tap the network you want to use**

If you see a padlock icon next to the network name, for instance 🔒 🛜 ⓘ, you will need a password to gain access to this network.

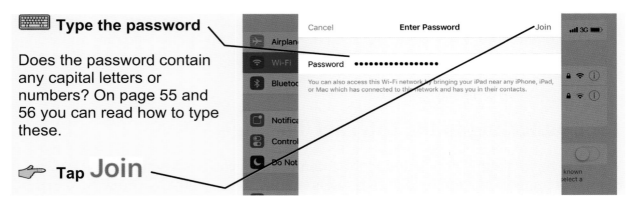

⌨ **Type the password**

Does the password contain any capital letters or numbers? On page 55 and 56 you can read how to type these.

☞ **Tap Join**

You will be connected to the wireless network:

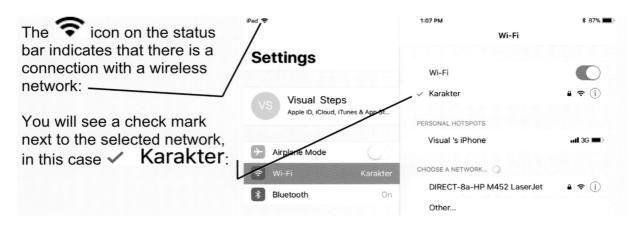

The 🛜 icon on the status bar indicates that there is a connection with a wireless network:

You will see a check mark next to the selected network, in this case ✓ **Karakter**:

In future, the connection with known wireless networks will be made automatically as soon as you enable Wi-Fi. You can check this out for yourself by disabling Wi-Fi first:

☞ **By** Wi-Fi, **tap**

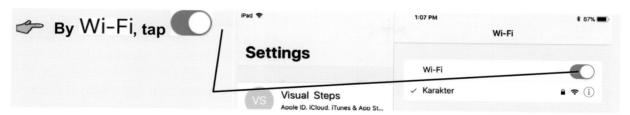

Now, Wi-Fi is disabled and you will see that the button looks like this ⬭. The 🛜 icon has disappeared from the status bar.

☞ **By** Wi-Fi, **tap**

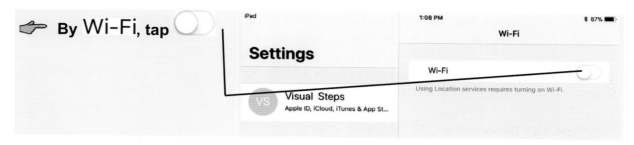

Wi-Fi will be enabled once again.

Automatically, the iPad will connect to the wireless network you were previously using:

🖝 **Press the Home button**

1.7 Connecting to the Internet Through the Mobile Data Network

If your iPad is also suitable for the mobile data network, you can connect it to a 3G or 4G network. The 4G network is available in the United States and most of the other countries. Connecting to the mobile data network can be useful when you are in a location where there is no Wi-Fi. You will need to have a nano SIM card with a data subscription or contract, or a prepaid mobile Internet card. If you do not (yet) have these items, you can just read through this section.

 Tip

Mobile Internet
Since the iPad does not have a simlock, you are free to select a mobile Internet provider. Many providers, such as AT&T, Verizon Wireless and British Telecom offer data subscriptions for the iPad, including a nano SIM card. For prepaid mobile Internet plans you can use Virgin Mobile USA, AT&T, Verizon and Vodafone, among others.
The prices and conditions are subject to regular changes. Check out the websites of various providers for more information.

The nano SIM card holder is located on the bottom right-hand side of the longer side.

Remove the nano SIM card tray, by using the SIM eject tool (included in the packaging):

If you do not have this tool, you can also use the end of a small paperclip.

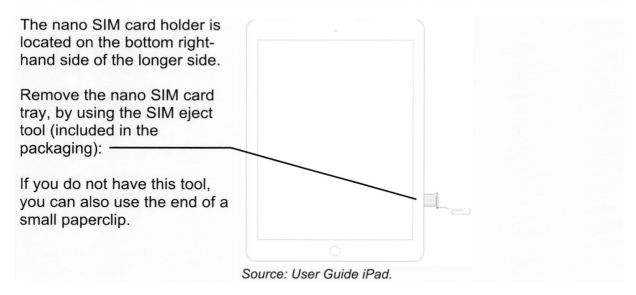

Source: User Guide iPad.

☞ **Place the nano SIM card in the SIM card tray**

☞ **Insert the nano SIM card tray into the iPad**

The connection with the mobile data network will start up automatically.

As soon as the connection has been made, you will see the signal strength and the name of the mobile network provider in use:

If the iPad status bar displays the 3G (**3G**) or 4G (**4G**), EDGE (**E**), or GPRS (**GPRS**) symbols, the device is connected to the Internet through the mobile data network.

If necessary, you can temporarily disable the Internet connection through the mobile data network. This way, you can prevent your children or grandchildren from playing online games on your iPad and using up all of your prepaid credit. Here is how to do that:

☞ **Open the *Settings* app**

☞ **Tap**  **Cellular Data**

☞ **By** Cellular Data, **tap**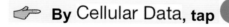

In the status bar, you will just see **iPad 📶**:

This means that there is no Internet connection through a mobile data network.

 Please note:

If you are using cellular data, by default, the Data roaming function will be disabled. *Data Roaming* means that you can use the network of a different Internet service provider, whenever the network of your own provider is out of reach. If you enable this option abroad, this may result in extremely high costs.

You can activate the cellular network again in the *Settings* app:

☞ **By** Cellular Data, **tap**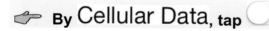

☞ **Press the Home button**

💡 **Tip**
Update for provider settings
You may see a message about an update for the carrier settings. These updates for carrier settings are small files (approximately 10 kB) that are downloaded and installed onto your iPad Wi-Fi + 3G or 4G.
The update is usually an improvement to the way in which your iPad connects to the data network of your provider (carrier). You should install the most recent updates for these carrier settings as soon as they are available.
☞ **Follow the onscreen instructions**

1.8 Putting the iPad to Sleep or Turning it Off

When you stop using the iPad, you can either turn it off or put it to sleep. When the iPad is in sleep mode, it is not turned off but will use less energy. If you have disabled Wi-Fi or the mobile data network, the iPad will use hardly any energy at all. This is how you put your iPad to sleep:

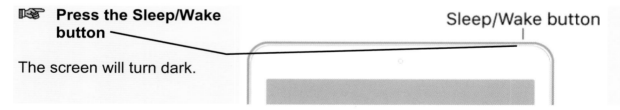

☞ **Press the Sleep/Wake button**

The screen will turn dark.

If you want to turn the iPad off completely, do this:

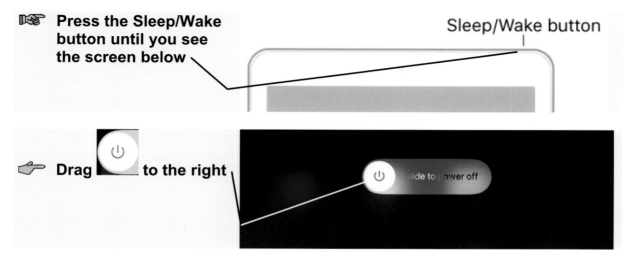

☞ **Press the Sleep/Wake button until you see the screen below**

☞ **Drag** ⏻ **to the right**

The screen will turn dark and the iPad is turned off. In future, you can decide whether you want to put the iPad in sleep mode, or turn it off.

In this chapter you have learned how to turn the iPad on and off and how to gain access to the Internet. You have also taken a closer look at some of the main components of the iPad and performed some basic operations for using the device.

 Tip

Set Touch ID
While you are working with the iPad, you may often be asked if you want to set the Touch ID. Apple recommends to use at least a passcode or Touch ID, to prevent unauthorized use of your iPad by others. You may still be asked to set the Touch ID, even if you have already entered a passcode. This is not necessary as such. In *section 7.3 Setting Up Touch ID* you can read how to set the Touch ID.

1.9 Background Information

Dictionary

AirDrop	A function that lets you quickly and easily share photos and other files with others next to you using Wi-Fi or Bluetooth.
Airplane mode	If your iPad is in this mode, you will not have access to the Internet and will not be able to use Bluetooth devices.
App	Short for *application*, a program for the iPad.
App icons	Colored icons on the iPad, used to open various apps.
App Store	Online store where you can download apps, for free or at a price.
Apple ID	Combination of an email address and a password. If you log in with an Apple ID you can use several options.
Bluetooth	Bluetooth is an open wireless technology standard for exchanging data over short distances. With Bluetooth you can connect a wireless keyboard or headset to the iPad, for example.
Control Center	In the *Control Center* you see the opened apps and frequently used functions. If you tap one of the buttons, the function is enabled or disabled. If the button is blue, the function is enabled.
Data roaming	Using the wireless network of another provider, when your own carrier's network is not available. Using this option abroad may lead to high costs.
Dock	Bar at the bottom of the home screen with frequently used apps. You can also open this bar from within an app, by dragging upwards from bottom to top.
EDGE	Short for *Enhanced Data Rates for GSM Evolution*. It allows improved data transmission rates as a backward-compatible extension of GSM. In the UK, EDGE coverage is reasonably widespread and in the USA it is pretty common.

- Continue on the next page -

GPRS	Short for *General Packet Radio Service*, a technology that is an extension of the existing gsm network. This technology makes it possible to transfer wireless data more efficiently, faster and cheaper.
Home button	⬭ , the button that lets you return to the home screen. You can also use this button to wake the iPad up from sleep.
Home screen	The screen with the app icons. This is what you see when you turn the iPad on or unlock it.
iPad	The iPad is a portable multimedia device (a tablet computer) made by Apple. The iPad is a computer with a multi-touch screen.
Location Services	Location services lets apps such as *Maps* gather and use data showing your location. For example, if you are connected to the Internet and have turned on location services, data about the location will be added to the photos and videos you take with your iPad.
Lock screen	The screen you see when you turn the iPad on. Before you can use the iPad, you need to unlock it.
Nano SIM card	The small SIM card that is used in the iPad Wi-Fi + 3G or 4G, for wireless data transfer. This SIM card is also called a 4FF SIM card (Fourth Form Factor).
Notification Center	A central option with which you can neatly arrange and display all the messages you have received on your iPad, such as new email messages and the notifications you have set up on your iPad. You can open this option by dragging across the screen from top to bottom.
Passcode	Code that provides access to your iPad.
Rotation lock	This function takes care of locking the screen display when you rotate the iPad.
Simlock	A simlock is a capability built into a cell phone or another wireless device that is used to restrict the use of the SIM card for that device. This lock prevents the user from using SIM cards from different providers in the device. The reason many network providers SIM lock their phones is that they offer phones at a discount to customers in exchange for a contract

- Continue on the next page -

	to pay for the use of the network for a specified time period, usually between one and three years. The iPad Wi-Fi + 3G or 4G is simlock free.
Sleep mode	You can lock the iPad by putting it into sleep mode if you do not use it for a while. When the iPad is locked, it will not react when you touch the screen. But you can still keep on playing music, for example. And you can still use the volume buttons. You can activate or deactivate sleep mode with the Sleep/Wake button.
Synchronize	Literally, this means: equalizing. If you sync your iPad with another device, the content of your iPad will be made equal to the content of that device.
Tablet computer	A tablet computer is a computer without casing and a separate keyboard. It is operated by a multi-touch screen.
Touch ID	Touch ID is the official name for the fingerprint scanner that you can use on the iPad. This way, you can secure your iPad by using your fingerprint.
Updating	Installing the latest version of the operating system or the last version of apps.
VPN	Short for *Virtual Private Network*. With VPN you can gain access to private secure networks through the Internet, such as your company network.
Wi-Fi	Wireless network for the Internet.
Widget	Widgets provide quick access to information, such as an appointment list, or the weather.
3G	3G is the third generation of standards and technology for cell phones. Because of its higher speed, 3G offers extensive possibilities. For example, with 3G you can use services such as making phone calls via the Internet, among others.
4G	4G is the fourth generation of standards and technology for cell phones. It is almost ten times the speed of 3G and will offer many new possibilities. 4G is available in the United States and most other countries.

Source: User Guide iPad, Wikipedia.

2. Sending Emails with Your iPad

Your iPad contains a standard email app called *Mail*.

With *Mail* you can send, receive and compose email messages, just like on your regular computer. In this chapter you can read how to adjust the settings for your email account. We will explain how to do this for Internet service providers (ISP), such as Sprint, T-Mobile, Cox, AT&T, US Cellular or Verizon, and also for web-based email services such as *Outlook.com* or *Hotmail*. If you use multiple email accounts, you can configure each one to work with the *Mail* program.

Composing an email on your iPad is quite easy. You will have lots of opportunity to practice this by working though this chapter. You will learn how to select, copy, cut, and paste items using the iPad screen. You will also become familiar with the auto-correct function that is built into the iPad.

Later on this chapter, we will explain how to send, receive and delete email messages. In the *Tips* at the back of the chapter you can read how to send an email with an attachment.

In this chapter you will learn how to:

- set up an email account;
- set up an *Outlook.com*, *Hotmail* or *Gmail* account;
- send an email;
- receive an email;
- reply to an email;
- move an email to the *Trash*;
- permanently delete an email.

2.1 Setting Up an Email Account

Before you can start sending emails, you need to adjust the settings on your iPad so that it can work with at least one email account. In this section, you can read how to do this for your own Internet service provider, such as Sprint, T-Mobile, Cox, AT&T, US Cellular or Verizon. To do this, you will need the information about the incoming and outgoing mail server, the user name and password given to you by your provider.

 Please note:

You may already have set up an email address while you were configuring your iPad. In this case, continue with *section 2.3 Typing and Sending an Email*.

☞ **If necessary, wake up the iPad from sleep mode or turn it on** 👣²

☞ **Open the *Settings* app** 👣¹

☞ **Drag upwards over the left side of the screen**

☞ **Tap**
🔑 **Accounts & Passw**

☞ **Tap**
Add Account

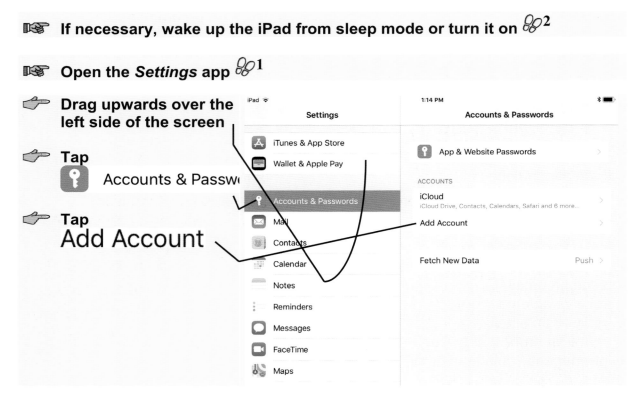

 Please note:

If you have a *Hotmail* account, you can skip this section and continue further in *section 2.2 Setting Up an Outlook.com, Hotmail or Gmail Account*.

You can choose from various well-known web-based providers. If you have an account with one of these popular providers, you only need your user name and password.

If your provider is not included in this list:

☞ **Tap** Other

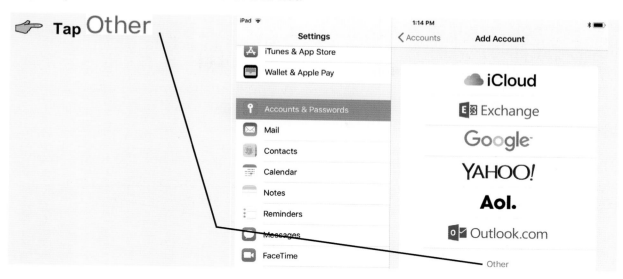

You can now add an email account:

☞ **Tap**
Add Mail Account

Now you will see a screen where you need to enter some basic information concerning your email account. To do this, you can use the onscreen keyboard from the iPad:

⌨ **By** Name**, type your name**

⌨ **By** Email**, enter your email address**

⌨ **By** Password**, type your password**

⌨ **By** Description**, type an identifiable name for your email account**

When you have finished entering the information:

☞ **Tap** Next

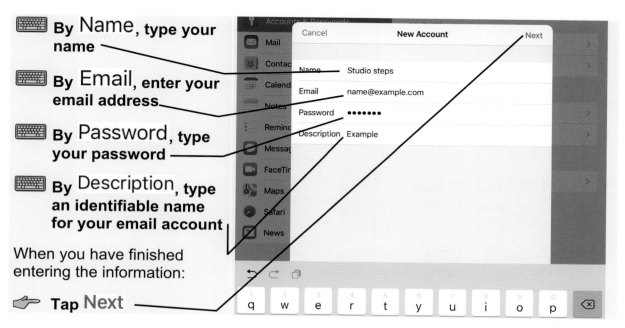

HELP! How do I type capital letters, numbers, and/or special symbols, such as @?

If your email address or password contains capital letters, numbers, and/or special symbols, you will read how to type these on page 55 and 56. The @ symbol is typed

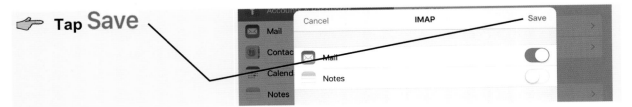

by tapping the .?123 key first, and then tapping @ .

The data you entered are checked. If these are correct, you will see the next screen:

☞ **Tap Save**

 HELP! It did not work.

If the data are not recognized or approved, you will see a new screen. Here you can enter more detailed data. You will probably have received these data from your email provider.

First, you need to choose whether you want to set up your email account according to the POP protocol or the IMAP protocol. We recommend IMAP, because then you can read your email on all the devices on which you use this function.

☞ **Tap IMAP**

By **INCOMING MAIL SERVER**:

⌨ By **Host Name type the name of the incoming mail server**

⌨ By **User Name type the user name**

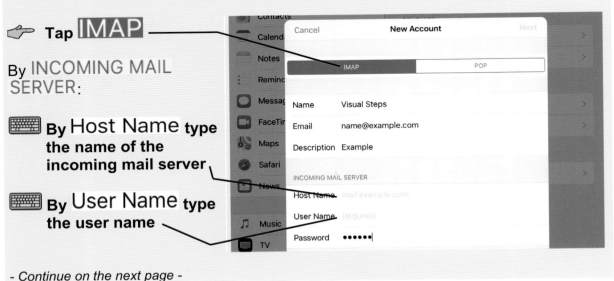

- Continue on the next page -

☞ **Drag your finger over the screen**

By OUTGOING MAIL SERVER:

⌨ **By** Host Name, **type the name of the outgoing mail server**

If by OUTGOING MAIL SERVER you see the text Optional in the fields for the user name and password, you do not need to enter this information.

☞ **Tap** Next

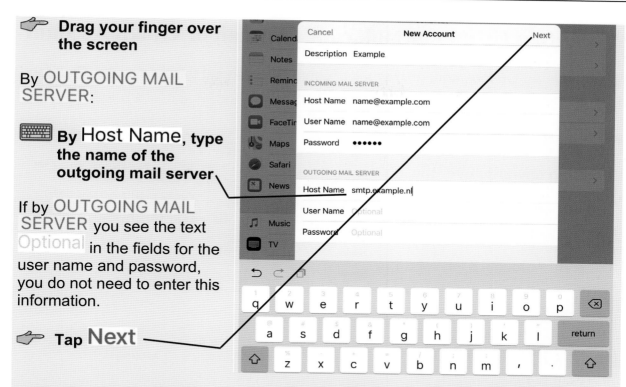

Does it still not work? Many providers such as AT&T and Cox have put instructions on their websites about setting up an email account for the iPad. Just look for something like 'email settings iPad' on your provider's website and follow the instructions listed.

Now your email account has been added:

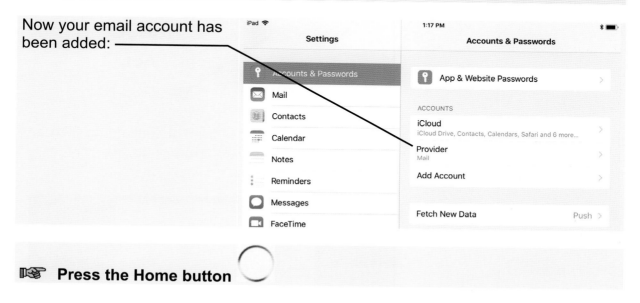

☞ **Press the Home button**

2.2 Setting Up an Outlook.com, Hotmail or Gmail Account

If you have an *Outlook.com* or *Hotmail* account, you can set this up on your iPad too. You can set up a *Gmail* account in a similar way.

☞ **Open the *Settings* app** ✂1

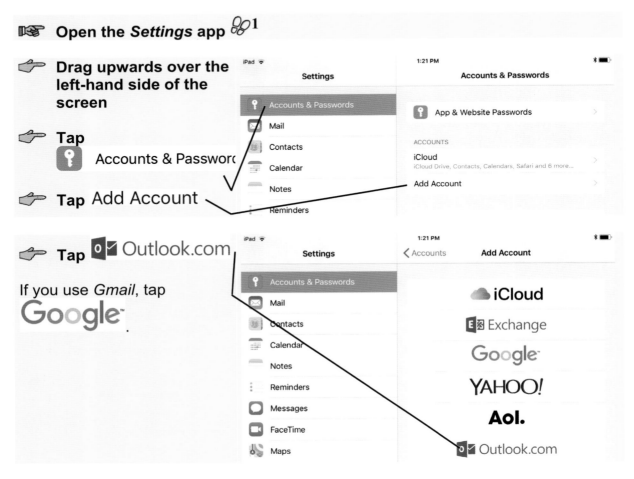

☞ **Drag upwards over the left-hand side of the screen**

☞ **Tap**

  🔑 Accounts & Passwords

☞ **Tap** Add Account

☞ **Tap** 📧 Outlook.com

If you use *Gmail*, tap

Google

In this example we have used an email address that ends with outlook.com. You can follow the same steps in case you want to use an email address ending in *hotmail.com*.

⌨ **By** Sign in**, type your email address**

☞ **Tap** Next

By Enter password**, type your password**

☞ **Tap** Sign in

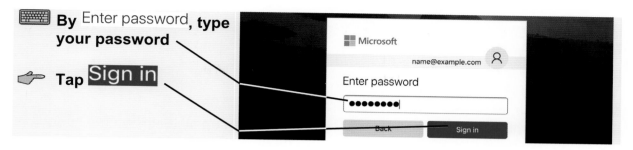

The iPad will recognize the server automatically. On the next page you give permission to some settings:

☞ **Tap** Yes

On this page you can select an option to synchronize your contacts and calendars too, besides your email. By default, these options are enabled:

☞ **Tap** Save

You will see that the account has been added:

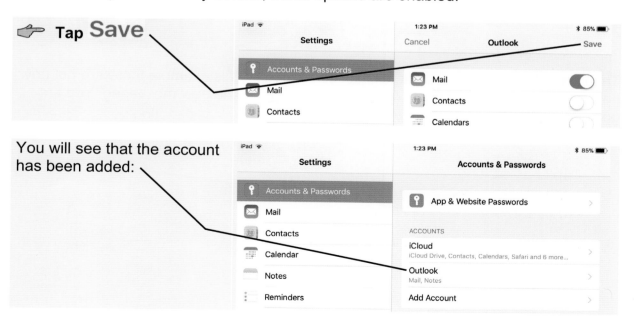

Press the Home button

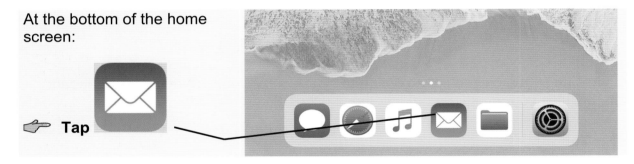

💡 **Tip**

Multiple email accounts
Do you have multiple email accounts? Then you can set up all these accounts on your iPad. Follow the steps in *section 2.1 Setting up an Email account*, or *2.2 Setting Up an Outlook.com, Hotmail or Gmail account* and execute the steps for each individual email account.

2.3 Typing and Sending an Email

Just for practice, you are going to write an email message to yourself. In this section you will also learn how to use the onscreen keyboard. You can put these actions to use in any app on the iPad.

First, you need to open the *Mail* app:

At the bottom of the home
screen:

☞ **Tap**

The app will immediately check for new messages. In this example there are not any new messages, but your own *Mail* app may contain some new messages. You are going to open a new, blank email:

☞ **Tap**

A new message will be opened.

By To:, type your email address

You will see the _____ key appear in the onscreen keyboard when you start typing in the To: field:

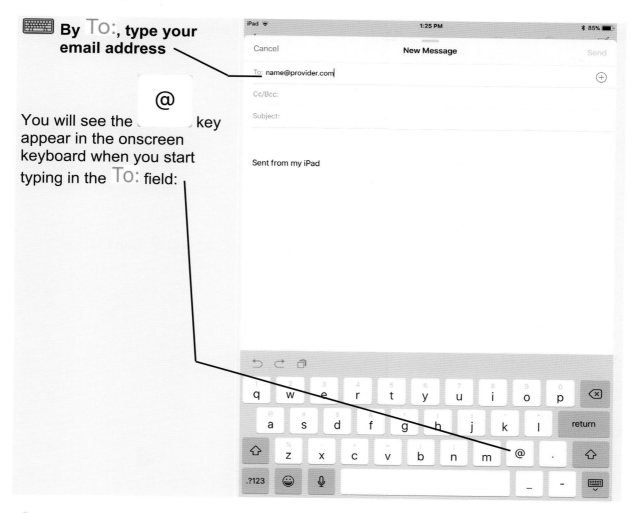

 Tip

Contacts

You can use the ⊕ button to open the list of contacts. You can select the recipient from this list by tapping his or her name.

In *Chapter 4 The Standard Apps and Functions* you will learn how to enter contacts in the list with the *Contacts* app.

☞ **Tap** Subject:

⌨ **Type:** Test

☞ **Tap the white area where you want to type your message**

⌨ **Type:** This is my

On the keyboard you will see some other signs above the gray letters, as you can see here q and h. You type these signs by dragging across the key from top to bottom. Just type the number 1:

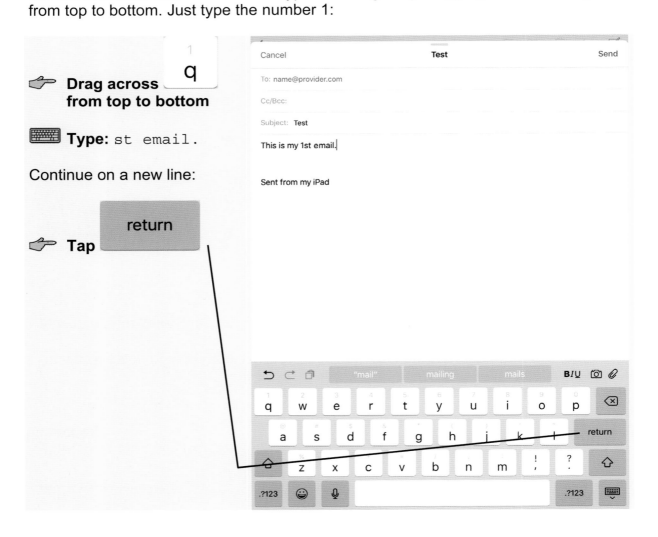

☞ **Drag across q from top to bottom**

⌨ **Type:** st email.

Continue on a new line:

☞ **Tap** return

Tip

Comma, period, exclamation mark, question mark

The comma and the exclamation mark share a key on the keyboard, just as the period and the question mark. This is how to type the symbol on the lower part of the key, for example, the period:

 **Tap**

And this is how to type the symbol on the upper part of the key, for example, the question mark:

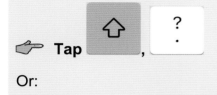 **Tap**

Or:

Drag from top to bottom

There are more views available for the onscreen keyboard. Just take a look at them:

Tap

The keyboard view will change:

You see some new characters:

If you tap **#+=** , you will see even more characters:

You will return to the standard view:

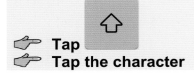 **Tap**

💡 **Tip**

Capital letters

New sentences will automatically begin with a capital letter. This is how to type a capital letter in the middle of a sentence:

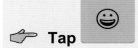 **Tap**

☞ **Tap the character**

💡 **Tip**

Emoticons

Emoticons (also called *smileys*) are used to convey an emotion. This is how you type them:

 Tap

☞ **Tap the desired emoticon, for example** 😊

Return to the regular keyboard view by tapping **ABC**.

💡 **Tip**

Backspace key

If you have typed the wrong text, you can correct this with the backspace key:

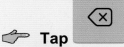 **Tap**

If you keep depressing this key, the words will be quickly deleted.

The iPad contains a dictionary that will help you while you are typing. Just see what happens when you intentionally make a spelling mistake:

Type: Type a speling

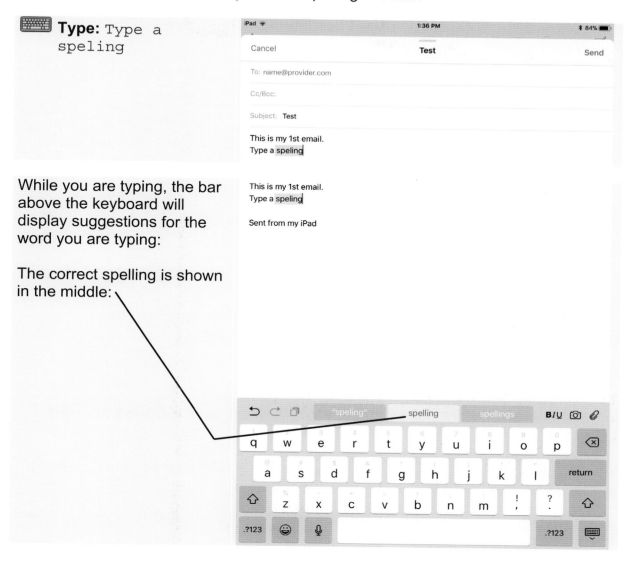

While you are typing, the bar above the keyboard will display suggestions for the word you are typing:

The correct spelling is shown in the middle:

You can accept the suggested correction without stopping, just continue typing:

Type a blank space

You will see that the mistake is corrected:

Type: mistake on the

Tip
Accept correction
A suggested correction will also be accepted if you type a period, comma or another punctuation symbol.

 Tip
Refuse correction
You can also refuse to accept a given suggestion. You do that like this:

 Tap the correction that is shown between the double quotes
"Maria"

You need to do this before you type a blank space, period, comma or other punctuation symbol, otherwise the correction will be accepted.

 Tip
Turn off Auto-Correct
In the *Tips* at the back of this chapter you can read how to disable the auto- correct function while typing.

You can also copy, cut and paste text. You can do this with an entire word, multiple words or the entire text. Here is how you select a word:

☞ **Press your finger on the word** iPad

Now you will see a magnifying glass with the selected word:

☞ **Release your finger**

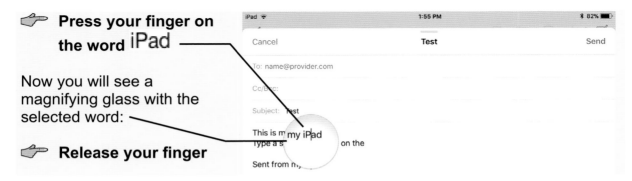

Now you can choose whether you want to select a single word or the entire text. You are going to select the word:

Tap **Select**

💡 **Tip**

Magnifying glass

With the magnifying glass, you can easily position the cursor on the exact spot inside a word, or between two words. This is helpful when you want to edit or correct text. Move your finger along, until you can see the correct position of the cursor in the magnifying glass, then release your finger. You will not need to use the **Select** or **Select All** buttons. You can just go on typing.

The word has been selected. To select multiple words, you can move the pins ┃ and ●. Now you can cut or copy it, or replace it by a similar word. You are going to copy the word:

Tap **Copy**

The word has been copied to the clipboard. This is how you paste it in the text:

👉 **Tap next to the second sentence**

⌨️ **Type a space**

👉 **Tap**

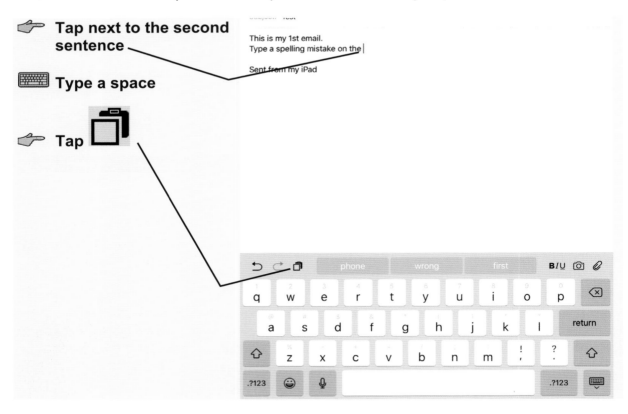

The copied word is pasted on the first line. It is also possible to format the text. For example, you can render words in bold or in italics.

👉 **Select the word '1st'** 👣3

👉 **Tap** **B***I*U̲

By tapping ▶ you can see more options, such as inserting a photo or video. In the *Tips* at the end of this chapter you can read more about this.

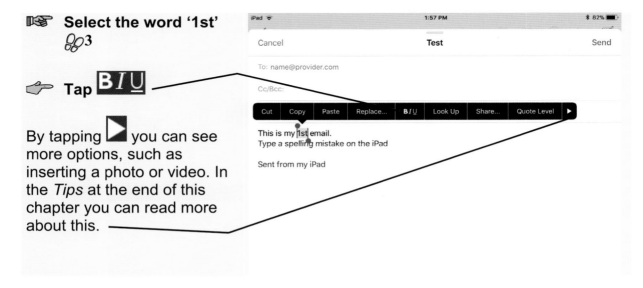

To render the word bold:

👉 **Tap** Bold

In the same way, you can render the text in italics, and underline it.

👉 **Tap next to the text**

💡 Tip

Formatting options on the keyboard

You can also use the formatting options on the keyboard. First you will need to select the format option. The text that you will type will have the selected format:

👉 **Tap** **B**_I_U

👉 **Tap the desired option**

When you type a text it will have the selected format.

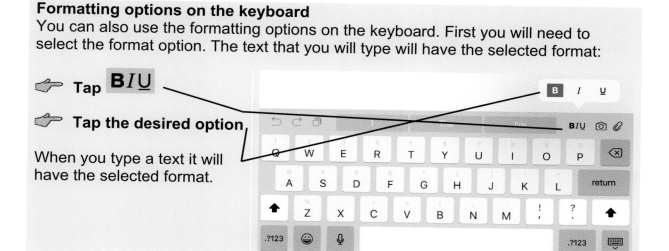

Now you can send your test email message:

👉 **Tap** Send

Your email message will be sent.

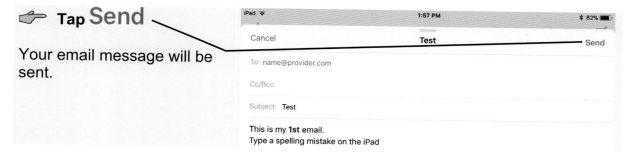

2.4 Receiving an Email

Shortly afterwards, your message will be received. You may hear another sound signal. This is how you open the *Inbox* folder, where your incoming messages are stored:

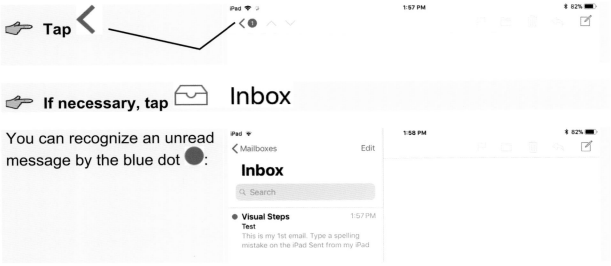

☞ **Tap**

☞ **If necessary, tap** Inbox

You can recognize an unread message by the blue dot ●:

HELP! I do not see a new message.

When you do not see a new email message:

☞ **Tap**
☞ **Swipe downwards over the left side of the screen**

At the bottom of the screen you will see this message: **Updated Just Now** 1 Unread . This means that the system has recently checked for new email messages.

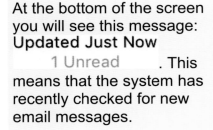

Tap the incoming message

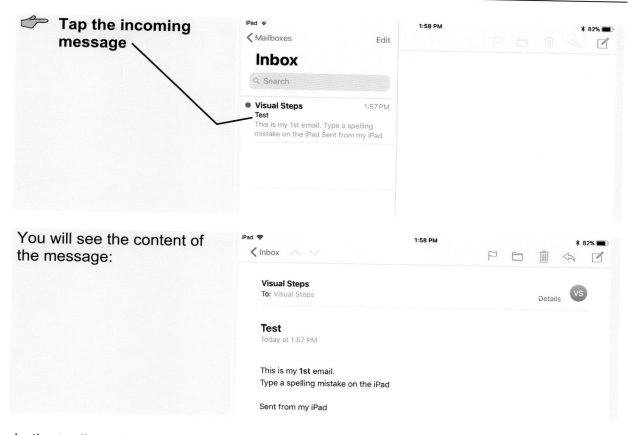

You will see the content of the message:

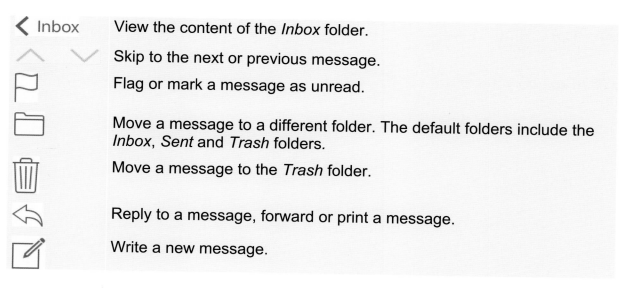

In the toolbar above a message you will find a few buttons. Here are the functions of these buttons:

❮ Inbox — View the content of the *Inbox* folder.

⌃ ⌄ — Skip to the next or previous message.

⚑ — Flag or mark a message as unread.

🗀 — Move a message to a different folder. The default folders include the *Inbox*, *Sent* and *Trash* folders.

🗑 — Move a message to the *Trash* folder.

↩ — Reply to a message, forward or print a message.

✎ — Write a new message.

2.5 Replying To an Email

This is how you reply to an email:

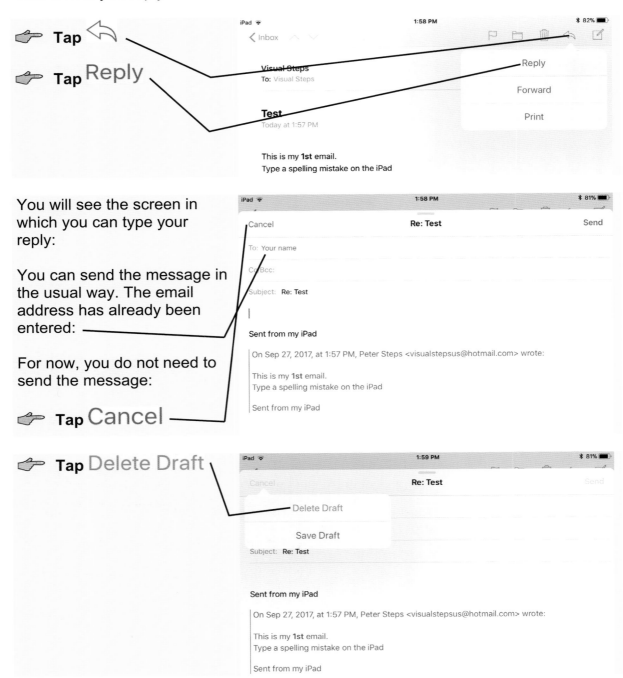

☞ Tap

☞ Tap Reply

You will see the screen in which you can type your reply:

You can send the message in the usual way. The email address has already been entered:

For now, you do not need to send the message:

☞ Tap Cancel

☞ Tap Delete Draft

You will see the screen again with the message you have previously sent to yourself.

2.6 Deleting an Email

You are going to delete your test message:

Now the email message has been moved to the *Trash* folder. You can check to make sure:

In this example there are no other messages in the *Inbox* folder:

If you have set up a single email account:

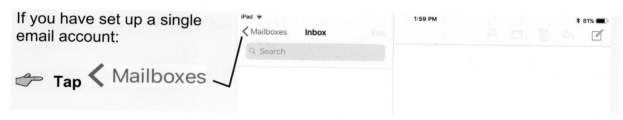

You will see a few folders:

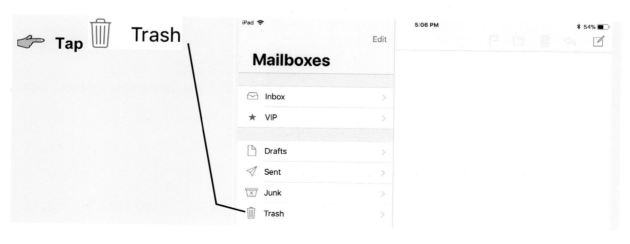

Please note:
If you have set up multiple email accounts, you need to tap the name of your account first before you see the *Trash* folder.

The deleted message is stored in the *Trash* folder. This is how you permanently delete the message:

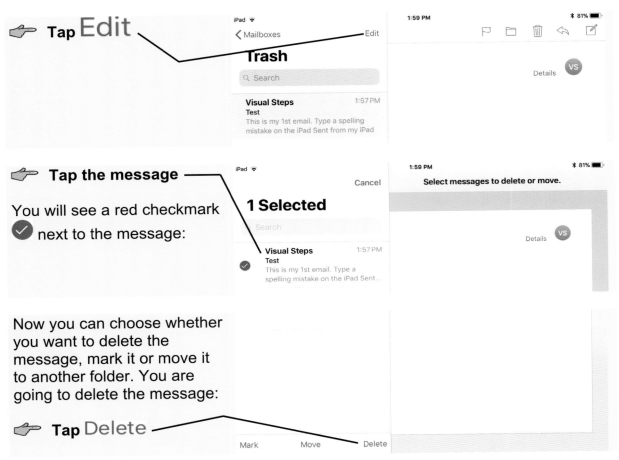

Tap Edit

Tap the message

You will see a red checkmark next to the message:

Now you can choose whether you want to delete the message, mark it or move it to another folder. You are going to delete the message:

Tap Delete

 Tip

Delete all messages
If you want to delete all messages, you do not need to tap the message. Instead tap Delete All. If you are sure, tap Delete All.

This is how you return to the *Inbox*:

 Tap < Mailboxes

 **Tap** ⬚ Inbox

Now you see your *Inbox* again.

Please note:

If you have set up multiple email accounts, your *Inbox* looks a bit different. You need to tap the name of your account first before you can tap the *Inbox*.

☞ **Press the Home button** ◯

In this chapter, you have set up an email account on the iPad, sent and received an email message and deleted an email. In the *Tips* you receive additional information, such as info on working with attachments, among other things.

2.7 Background Information

Dictionary

Account   A combination of a user name and password that gives you access to a specific protected service. A subscription with an Internet service provider is also called an account.

Attachment   A file that can be linked to an email message and sent along with it. This can be a document, picture, or another type of file.

Auto-Correct   This function automatically corrects misspelled words.

Contacts   Standard app on the iPad with which you can view and edit the information about your contacts.

Gmail   Free email service provided by the manufacturers of the well-known *Google* search engine.

IMAP   IMAP stands for *Internet Message Access Protocol*. This means that you manage your emails on the mail server. Messages that you have read, will be stored on the mail server until you delete them. IMAP is useful if you want to manage your email from multiple computers. Your mailbox will look the same on all the computers you use. If you create folders to organize your email messages, these same folders will appear on each computer, as well as on your iPad. If you want to use IMAP, you will need to set up your email account as an IMAP account on every device you use.

Inbox   Folder in *Mail* where you can view the email messages you have received.

Mail   Standard app on the iPad with which you can send and receive email messages.

Outlook.com   Free email service of Microsoft.
(Hotmail)

- Continue on the next page -

POP   POP stands for *Post Office Protocol*, the traditional method of managing your emails. When you retrieve your email, the messages will be deleted from the server right away. But on your iPad, the default setting for POP accounts is for saving a copy on the mail server, even after you have retrieved the message. This means you will also be able to retrieve the same message on other devices.

Signature   Standard ending that will be inserted at the end of all your outgoing emails.

Trash   Folder in *Mail* where all your deleted messages are stored. Once you have deleted a message from the *Trash*, it will be deleted permanently.

Source: User Guide iPad, Wikipedia.

2.8 Tips

Tip
Enable Caps Lock
If you only want to use capitals:

☞ **Double-tap**

The key will turn into ____. Now you will only see capital letters when you type something.

To return to the normal operation of this key:

☞ **Tap**

Tip
Letters with accent marks
You will not find letters with accent marks on the onscreen keyboards. But you can still type them:

☞ **For example, press the** e **key**

You will see a small window with various accents marks for the letter e, such as é and è.

☞ **Move your finger from the** e **key to the e key with the accent mark you want to use**

Please note: when you release the e key first, the window will disappear.

☞ **Release the key**

The e with the accent mark will appear in the text.

Tip

Type faster

This is how you can quickly type a period and a blank space at the end of a sentence:

☞ **Double-tap the space bar twice, quickly**

 Tip

Disable Auto-Correct

Sometimes, the auto-correct function on the iPad will insert unwanted corrections. The dictionary will not recognize every single word you type, but will try to suggest a correction, nevertheless. This may result in strange corrections, which you might accept without knowing it, whenever you type a period, comma or blank space. This is how to disable the auto-correct function:

☞ **Open the *Settings* app** 𝒢𝒢¹

☞ **If necessary, tap** ⚙ **General**

☞ **Tap** Keyboard

☞ **By** Auto-Correction, **tap the** ⬤ **button**

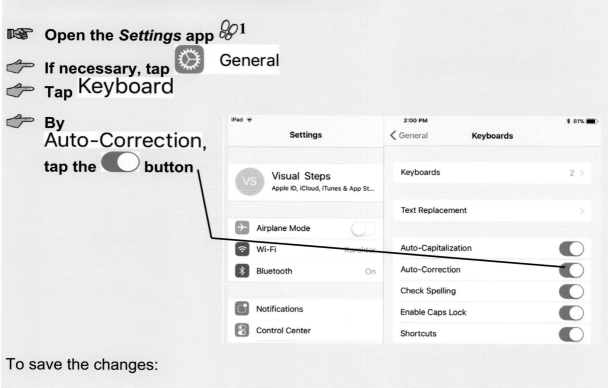

To save the changes:

☞ **Press the Home button**

Tip

Adding an attachment

You can send an attachment such as a photo or short video with your email message. In this example a photo is being sent. In *Chapter 6 Photos and Video* you can learn more about working with photos and video.

☞ **Open a new email message** 🐾4

☞ **Press your finger to the message**

When you see the magnifying glass:

☞ **Release your finger**

☞ **Tap**
Insert Photo or Vi

☞ **Tap the folder with the photo, for example** Moments
☞ **Tap the picture**
☞ **Tap** Use

The photo will be added to the email.

If you have other types of documents such as a text file or a PDF file stored on your iPad, you can send these as attachments as well. You do this by opening the document with the app you normally use to view or edit the document. For PDFs this can be *iBooks* for example. Once the document is opened, tap ⬆️ and Mail. You can also tap 📎 in the window of a new email message.

Tip

Opening an attachment received in an email

Once in a while, you will receive a message with an attachment. This can be in the form of a photo, video or other type of document such as a PDF file. Most of these types of files can be opened directly on your iPad. In this tip is shown how to open a *Word* document that has been received as an attachment to an email. For other types of files, the procedure is pretty much the same.

☞ **Open the email message with the attachment** ✇5

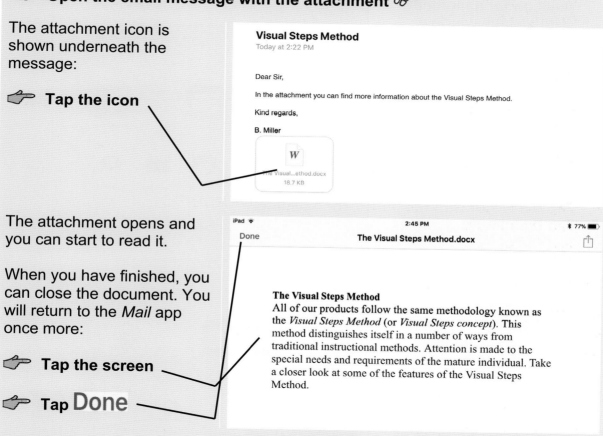

The attachment icon is shown underneath the message:

☞ **Tap the icon**

The attachment opens and you can start to read it.

When you have finished, you can close the document. You will return to the *Mail* app once more:

☞ **Tap the screen**

☞ **Tap Done**

- Continue on the next page -

If desired, you can use this document with other apps or even print it. To do this, you

click ⬆️ and select one of the options shown.

If you have received a document that you want to open in a specific app, such as *iBooks* for a PDF file, then you need to select the app from the list of available options shown.

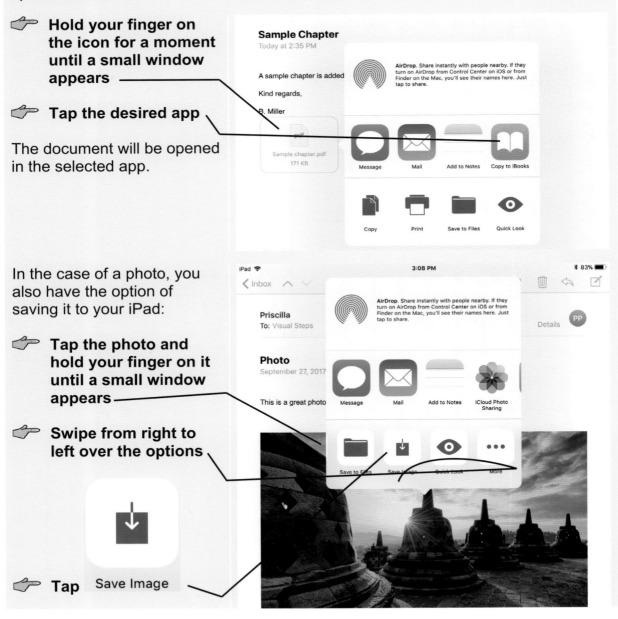

☞ **Hold your finger on the icon for a moment until a small window appears**

☞ **Tap the desired app**

The document will be opened in the selected app.

In the case of a photo, you also have the option of saving it to your iPad:

☞ **Tap the photo and hold your finger on it until a small window appears**

☞ **Swipe from right to left over the options**

☞ **Tap** Save Image

Tip

Choosing a sender
If you have multiple email accounts setup on your iPad, you can decide from which sender an email message is sent.

 **Tap** Cc/Bcc:
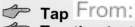 **Tap** From:
 Tap the desired email address

 Tip

iPad horizontal
If you hold the iPad in a horizontal position, by default, you will see your mailbox with email messages on your screen:

The mailbox with the messages:

The email message:

When a new email message is opened, the keys on the keyboard are also displayed in a larger size.

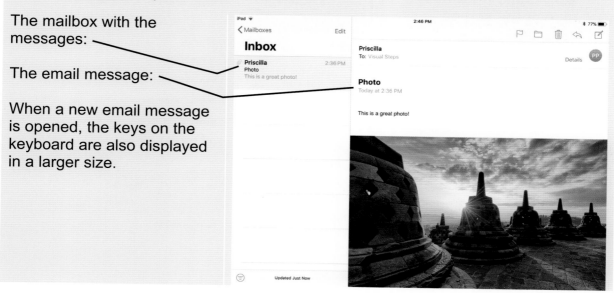

Tip

Signature

By default, each email you send will end with the text *Sent from my iPad.* This text is called your *signature*. You can replace this text by a standard ending for your messages or by your name and address. This is how to change your email signature:

☞ **Open the *Settings* app** ✌¹

👉 **Tap** ✉ **Mail**

👉 **If necessary, swipe across the right-hand side of the screen**

👉 **Tap** Signature

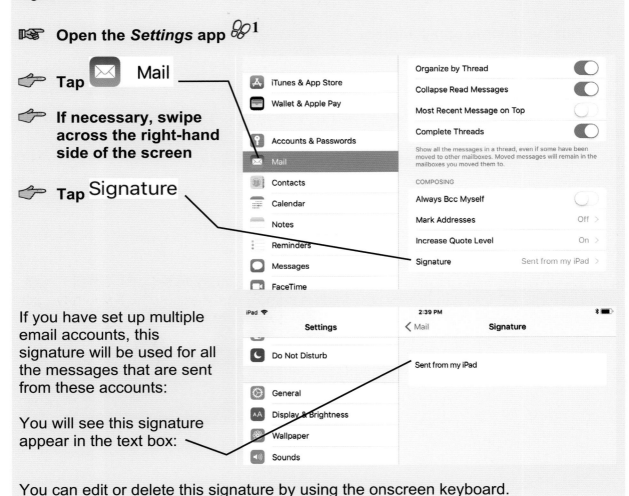

If you have set up multiple email accounts, this signature will be used for all the messages that are sent from these accounts:

You will see this signature appear in the text box:

You can edit or delete this signature by using the onscreen keyboard.

Tip

CC/BCC

The screen in which you can type a new email message also contains the Cc/Bcc: field. With CC (*Carbon Copy*) and BCC (*Blind Carbon Copy*) you can send others a copy of your message. The recipients in the BCC field will not be visible to the other recipients of this message. But if you use the CC field, every recipient can view the other recipients.

 Tap Cc/Bcc:

Now you will see both options apart from each other. You can type the email addresses in the fields.

 Tip

Moving email messages to folders

You can also move your emails to different folders. If you have set your email account to IMAP, you can create new folders in most email accounts. If you have not yet created folders, you can do this in the *Mailboxes* window:

 Tap Edit

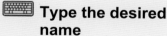 **At the bottom, tap** New Mailbox

 **Type the desired name**

By MAILBOX LOCATION you can choose a location, if you wish:

When you are done:

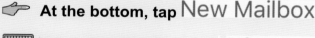 **Tap** Save

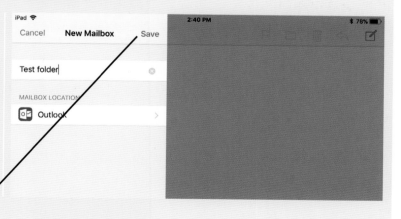

- Continue on the next page -

In the next screen, you will see the new folder:

👉 Tap **Done**

This is how you move an email:

👉 **Open an email message** 👣5

👉 **Tap** 📁

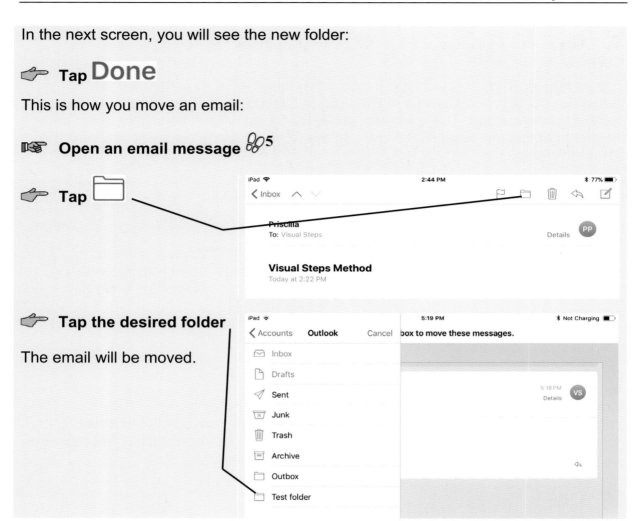

👉 **Tap the desired folder**

The email will be moved.

3. Surfing with Your iPad

In this chapter you are going to get acquainted with *Safari*, the web browser used by all Apple devices. With this web browser you can surf the Internet using your iPad. If you are familiar with using the Internet on your computer, you will see that surfing on the iPad is just as easy. The big difference is that you do not need a mouse, or keyboard to navigate. You surf by using the touchscreen on your iPad.

You will learn how to open a web page, zoom in and out and how to scroll by touching the screen in a specific way. We will also discuss how to open a *link* (or *hyperlink*) and work with web pages that you have saved, also called *bookmarks*.

In *Safari* you can open multiple web pages at a time. In this chapter you will learn how to switch back and forth between these open pages.

In this chapter you will learn how to:

- open a web page;
- zoom in and zoom out;
- scroll;
- open a link on a web page and on a new tab;
- switch between multiple open page tabs;
- go to the previous or next page;
- add a bookmark;
- search.

 Please note:

In this chapter you will practice the operations with the Visual Steps website. This website is modified and renewed on a regular basis. That is why you may see screens that look a bit different. In such a case you should just try to execute the operations. If this is not possible, you can try to execute the operations in another part of the web page.

3.1 Opening a Web Page

This is how you open *Safari*, the app that allows you to surf the Internet:

☞ **If necessary, wake up the iPad from sleep mode or turn it on** $\mathscr{O}^2$

☞ **Tap**

To practice, you can take a look at the Visual Steps website. This is to how to display the onscreen keyboard, in order to enter the web address:

☞ **Tap the address bar**

⌨ **Type:**
www.visualsteps
.com

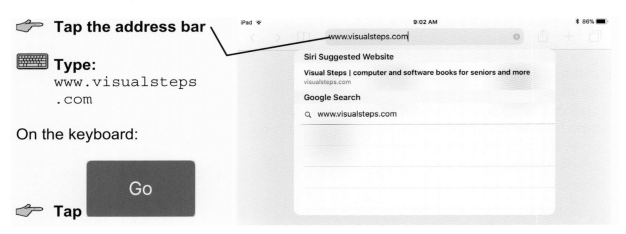

On the keyboard:

☞ **Tap** Go

HELP! A web address is already entered.
If another web address is shown in the address bar, you can delete it like this:

☞ **Tap**

Now you will see the Visual Steps website:

3.2 Zoom In and Zoom Out

If you think that the letters and images on a website are too small, you can zoom in. This is done by double-tapping. Tap the desired spot twice, in rapid succession:

☞ Double-tap the menu on the left-hand side

HELP! A new web page is opened.

If you do not double-tap in the right way, a new tab might be opened. If that is the case, just tap ⟨ on the screen at the top left and try again. You can also practice double-tapping in a blank area of your screen.

You will see that the web page is rendered in a larger size:

☞ **Double-tap the menu once more**

Now the screen will zoom out to the standard view again. There is also another way to zoom in and out; sort of like pinching. You use your thumb and index finger:

☞ **Slowly spread your thumb and index finger away from each other on the screen**

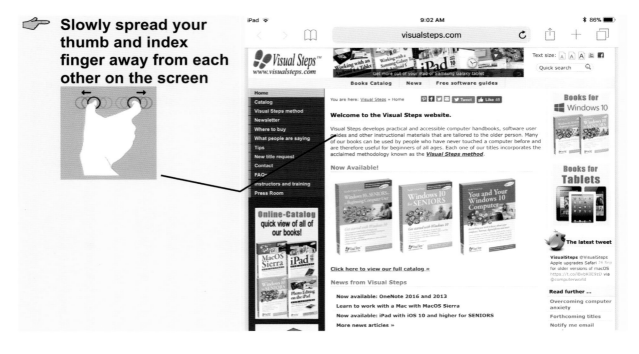

You will see that you can zoom in even further. It will take a moment for the screen to focus. You can zoom out by reversing the movement of your fingers:

☞ **Move your thumb and index finger towards each other on the screen**

You will see the normal view of the web page again. If you rotate the iPad a quarter turn, you will also see the web page in a larger size.

☞ **Turn the iPad to the left towards the horizontal position (landscape)**

3.3 Scrolling

Scrolling allows you to view the entire content of the web page. You scroll up or down to see more of the page. On your iPad, you do this with your fingers:

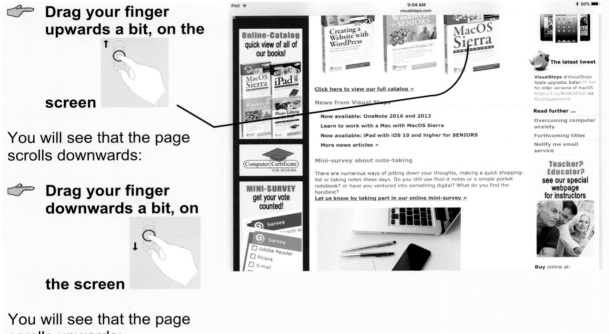

☞ **Drag your finger upwards a bit, on the screen**

You will see that the page scrolls downwards:

☞ **Drag your finger downwards a bit, on the screen**

You will see that the page scrolls upwards:

  Tip

Scrolling sideways
You can scroll sideways by moving your finger from right to left, or from left to right. On some websites this is only possible if you have zoomed in.

If you want to quickly scroll a longer page, you can swipe your finger over the screen:

☞ **Move your finger upwards in a swiping gesture, over the screen**

You will see that you will quickly scroll down to the bottom of the page:

Tip

Moving in different directions

You can also quickly scroll upwards, to the left, or to the right, if you swipe the screen in that direction. On some websites this is only possible if you have zoomed in.

This is how you quickly return to the top of the web page:

☞ **Tap the status bar twice**

At once, you will jump to the top of the web page:

☞ **Turn the iPad to the right towards the vertical position (portrait)**

3.4 Opening a Link on a Web Page

If a page contains a (hyper)link, you can follow this link by tapping it. Just try this:

☞ Tap **Catalog**

 HELP! Tapping the link does not work.

If you find it difficult to tap the right link, you can zoom in more. This way, the links will be displayed in a much larger format, and tapping the link will be easier.

Now the catalog will be opened, where you can view the Visual Steps books:

Here you see that the new page is displayed in the regular size:

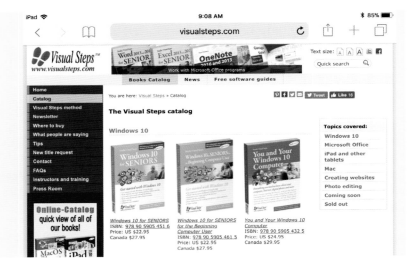

3.5 Opening a Link in a New Tab

You can also open a link in a new tab:

☞ **Put your finger on Where to buy**

HELP! Tapping the link does not work.
If you find it difficult to tap the right link, you can zoom in first. This way, the links will be displayed in a much larger format, and tapping the link will be easier.

In a few seconds, you will see a menu:

☞ **Tap Open in New Tab**

To open the new tab:

☞ **Tap the second tab**

Where to find our pr

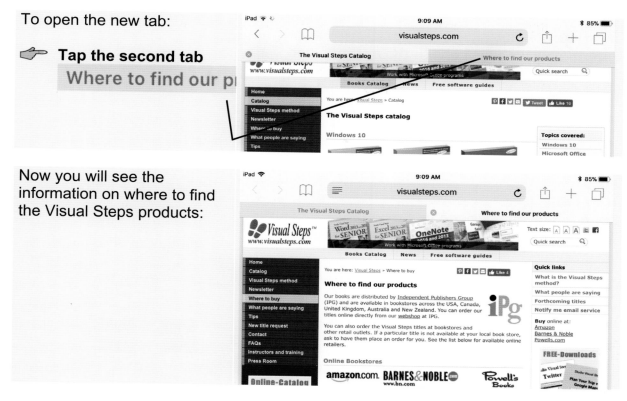

Now you will see the information on where to find the Visual Steps products:

You will close the opened tab:

☞ **Tap** ⊗

Now you see the catalog with Visual Steps books:

Tip
Enter a new web address in the address bar
If you want to type a new address in the address bar, you can remove the web address of the open web page in the following way:

 Tap the address bar

 **Tap**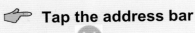

 Tip
Open a new, blank page in a new tab
This is how you open a new, blank page in *Safari*:

You will see a new tab:

☞ **Tap the address bar**

The onscreen keyboard will be opened. Now you can enter a web address.

When you have accidently closed a tab you can open it again by using ╬. Tap ╬ and hold your finger on it for a moment until you see the *Recently Closed Tabs* window. You can open the tab again by tapping one of the items shown.

3.6 Go to Previous or to Next Page

You can return to the web page you have previously visited. Here is how to do that:

You will again see the Visual Steps home page. You can also skip to the next page. To do this, you use the ╱ button, but right now this will not be necessary.

3.7 Adding a Bookmark

If you want to visit a page more often, you can make a bookmark for this page. A bookmark is a favorite website which you want to visit again, later on. In this way, you do not need to type the full web address every time you want to visit the site. This is how you add a bookmark:

☞ **Tap** 📤

A menu appears:

☞ **Tap** Add Bookmark

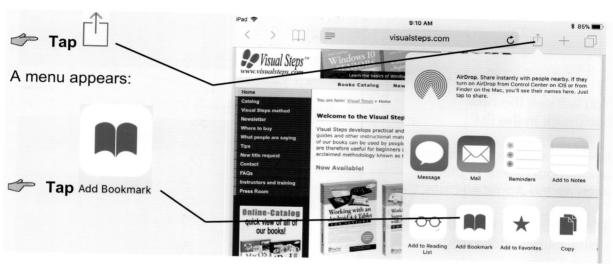

In the *Add Bookmark* window you can type an identifiable name for the web page. For now, this is not necessary.

In this example the bookmark will be saved in the Favorites section. The other section is Bookmarks. You change it by tapping the current location and then the other location. You do not need to do that now.

☞ **Tap** Save

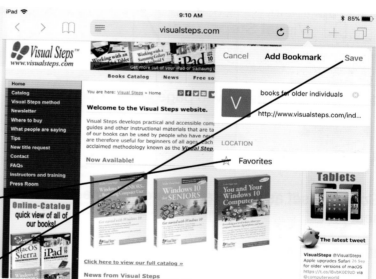

3.9 Background Information

Dictionary

Address bar	Bar in which you type the web address.
Bookmark	A link to a web address that has been stored in a list, so you can easily find the web page later on.
Google	Search engine of Google.
History	In the browser history, the links are saved to all the websites you have recently visited.
Hyperlink	A hyperlink is a navigation tool on a web page, which will automatically lead the user to the information when it is tapped. A hyperlink can be displayed in text or in an image, such as a photo, a button or an icon. Also called *link*.
Link	A different name for a hyperlink.
Reading list	In this list, you can save web pages that you want to view again later on. Then you will not need an Internet connection. The web pages will be removed from the list after you have opened them through the reading list.
Safari	Web browser manufactured by Apple.
Safari Reader	*Safari Reader* removes all the adverts and other elements that can distract you while you are reading online articles.
Scroll	Moving a web page on the screen upwards, downwards, to the left, or to the right. To do this on the iPad you need to touch the screen in a certain way.
Zoom in	Take a closer look at an item; the letters and images will become larger.
Zoom out	Look at an item from a distance; the letters and images will become smaller.

Source: iPad User Guide, Wikipedia.

3.10 Tips

💡 Tip

Delete a bookmark

If you no longer want to use a bookmark, you can delete it. Here is how to do that:

☞ **Tap** 📖

☞ **If necessary, tap** ☆ **Favorites**
☞ **At the bottom of the screen, tap** Edit

☞ **Tap** ⊖ **, next to the bookmark you want to delete**

☞ **Tap** Delete

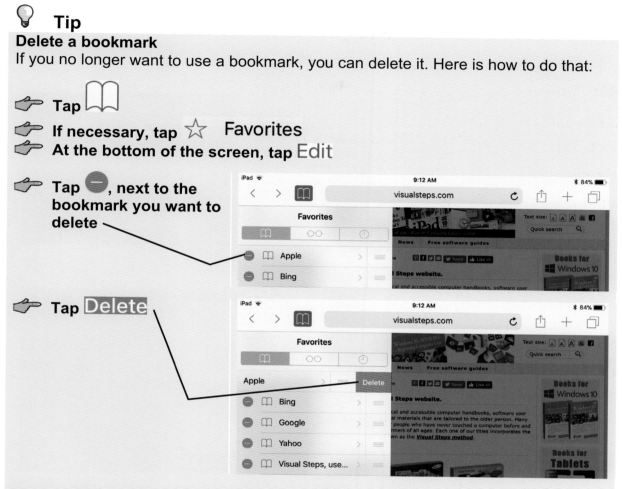

Please note: you can also drag your finger horizontally across the bookmark and then tap Delete.

The bookmark has been deleted:

You can close the window:

At the bottom of the *Favorites* window:

☞ **Tap** Done

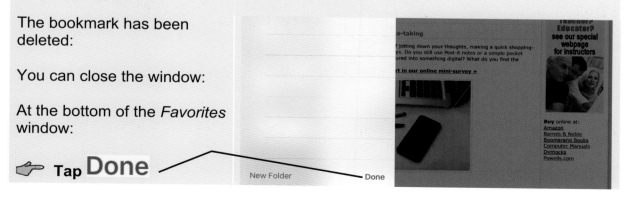

💡 Tip

View and delete history
In the history, all recently visited websites are stored. This is how you can view the history:

👉 **Tap** 📖

👉 **Tap** 🕐

You will see the visited websites.

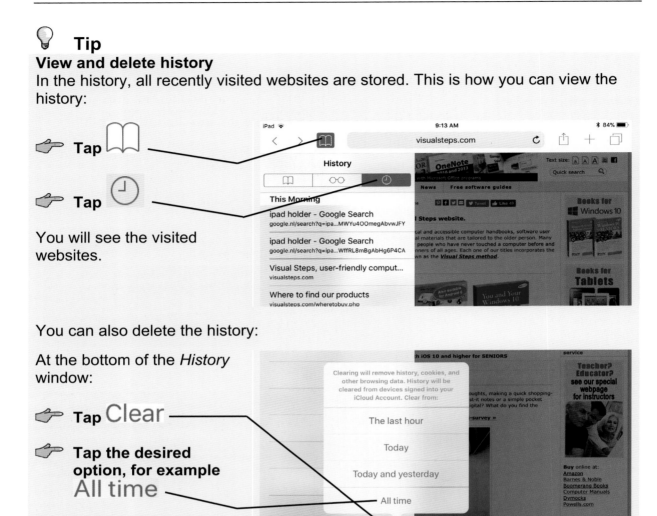

You can also delete the history:

At the bottom of the *History* window:

👉 **Tap** Clear

👉 **Tap the desired option, for example** All time

The history will be deleted.

Tip

Creating a reading list
In *Safari* you can create a reading list. A reading list contains links to web pages you want to visit at a later time. For that, you do not need an Internet connection.
This is how you add the current page to a reading list:

☞ **Tap** ⬆️

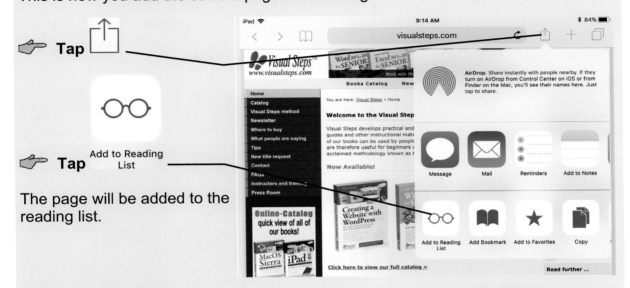

☞ **Tap** Add to Reading List

The page will be added to the reading list.

You are asked whether you would like to save reading list articles for offline reading automatically:

☞ **Tap**
Save Automatically

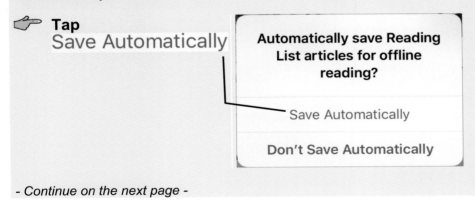

- Continue on the next page -

You can also add a link to the reading list like this:

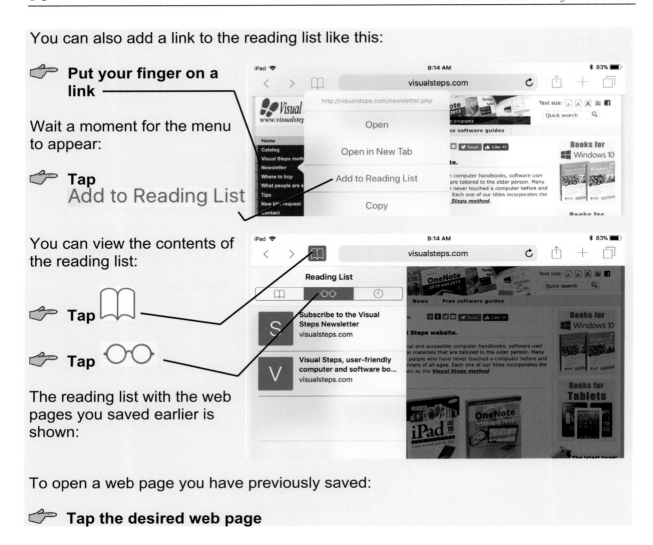

☞ **Put your finger on a link**

Wait a moment for the menu to appear:

☞ **Tap**
Add to Reading List

You can view the contents of the reading list:

☞ **Tap** 📖

☞ **Tap** 👓

The reading list with the web pages you saved earlier is shown:

To open a web page you have previously saved:

☞ **Tap the desired web page**

Tip

Safari Reader

Safari Reader will remove advertisements and other elements that may distract you while reading articles online. This option will only be displayed if a web page contains an article.

In this example you will see all sorts of advertorials above the article:

Safari has noticed that an article is displayed on this web page. You can tell this by the ≡ button in the address bar:

☞ **Tap** ≡

Now the article will be opened in a new window. You can read the article without being distracted.

The ≡ button has now turned black ▮. You can close the *Safari Reader* screen by tapping ▮:

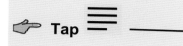

Notes

Write your notes down here.

4. The Standard Apps and Functions

Along with *Mail* and *Safari*, there are other useful apps already installed on your iPad. The *Contacts* app allows you to manage your contacts.

The *Calendar* app lets you keep track of your appointments and daily activities. Next to the *Calendar* app, the *Reminders* app will help you save important tasks.

In the *Maps* app you can look up addresses and well-known places. You can view these locations on a regular map or on a satellite photo. Once you have found the desired location, you can also get directions on how to get there. With this, you can even use your iPad with Wi-Fi and 3G/4G as a navigation system.

The iPad has a search utility. With this utility you can search through the apps, files, activities and contacts stored on your iPad. Another helpful function is *Siri*. *Siri* lets you give verbal instructions for the iPad to execute, and lets you ask the iPad for information.

In this chapter you will learn how to:

- add contacts in the *Contacts* app;
- add an activity in the *Calendar* app;
- set a reminder;
- work with the *Maps* app;
- use the *Notes* app;
- search on the iPad;
- ask *Siri* for help.

4.1 Adding a Contact

You can open the *Contacts* app on the home screen of your iPad.

☞ **If necessary, wake the iPad up from sleep or turn it on** ♘²

👉 **Tap** Contacts

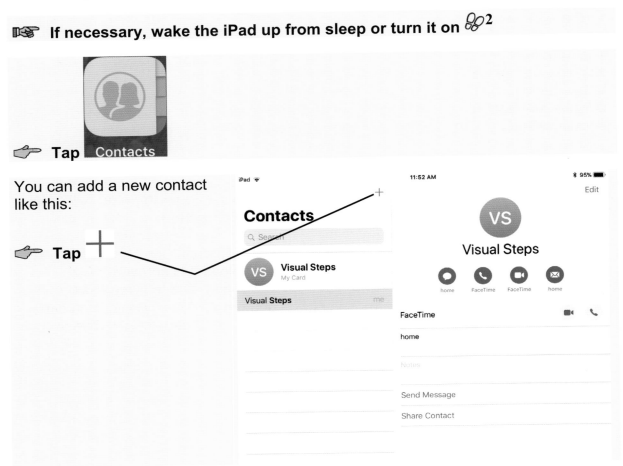

You can add a new contact
like this:

👉 **Tap ＋**

In this example we will add a fictitious contact. Of course, you can also enter the data for your own contact. Enter the desired data by tapping the corresponding field, and typing the data:

⌨ **Type the first name of
your contact**

👉 **Tap** Last name

⌨ **Type the last name of
your contact**

You can choose which data you enter. In this example, a phone number is added as well:

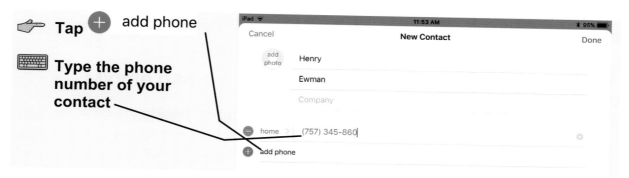

☞ **Tap** ➕ add phone

⌨ **Type the phone number of your contact**

🖐 **Please note:**

When you enter a phone number, the digits will automatically be grouped in the right order, including parentheses, dashes or no dashes as needed. The format used depends on the region format settings in the *Settings* app.

As soon as you start entering a phone number in a field, a new line will appear where you add another phone number. This will also happen when you enter data in other fields. The default label for the first phone number field is home . You can change the name of this label and other labels as well, for example in mobile or work.

☞ **Tap** home

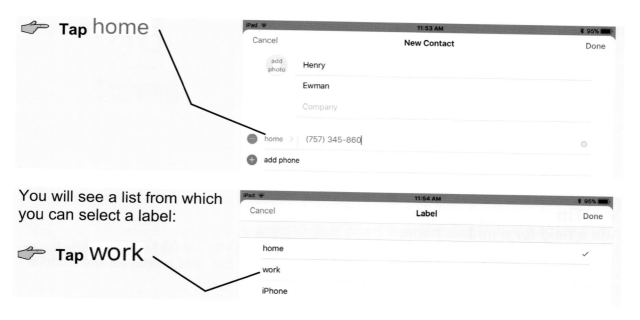

You will see a list from which you can select a label:

☞ **Tap** work

The calendar opens showing the current date and time.

In the Day view you can select a different date here:

If you have selected a different date from the current date, you can use the Today button to quickly return to your current appointments:

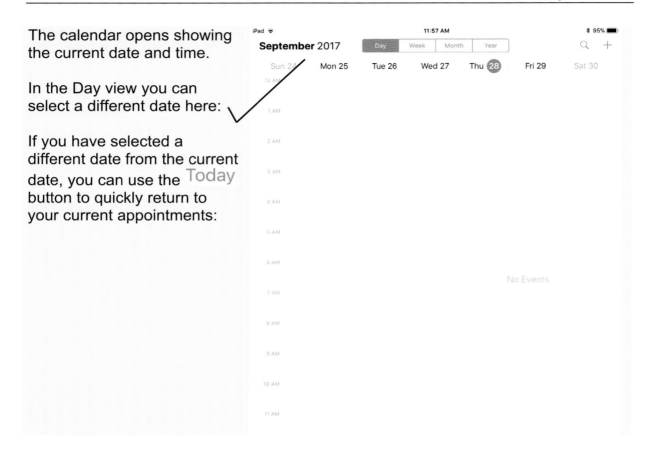

First, you check if the right calendar is displayed in the app:

☞ **Tap** Calendars

In this example you see several calendars. Depending on the accounts you have set up, for example, for *Hotmail*, you may also see other calendars.

This is how you select a calendar:

☞ **By** ON MY IPAD, **tap**
   • Calendar

☞ **Tap** Done

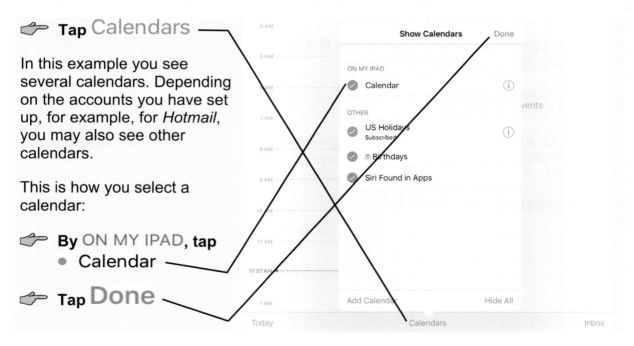

You can choose which data you enter. In this example, a phone number is added as well:

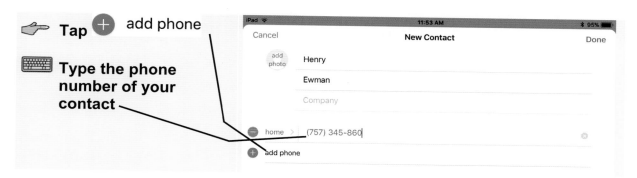

☞ **Tap** ⊕ add phone

⌨ **Type the phone number of your contact**

➥ **Please note:**

When you enter a phone number, the digits will automatically be grouped in the right order, including parentheses, dashes or no dashes as needed. The format used depends on the region format settings in the *Settings* app.

As soon as you start entering a phone number in a field, a new line will appear where you add another phone number. This will also happen when you enter data in other fields. The default label for the first phone number field is home. You can change the name of this label and other labels as well, for example in mobile or work.

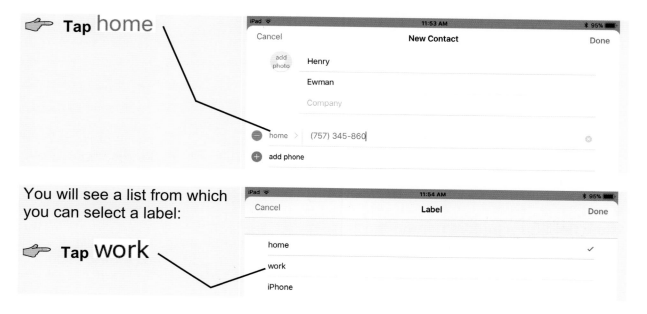

☞ **Tap** home

You will see a list from which you can select a label:

☞ **Tap** work

You can enter a lot of other information about your contact. It is up to you to fill in all the fields, or leave them blank.

 Add more information, if you wish 6

 Tip
Delete a field
If you want to delete a field that has been added, you tap ⊗ beside the data.

You will save your contact:

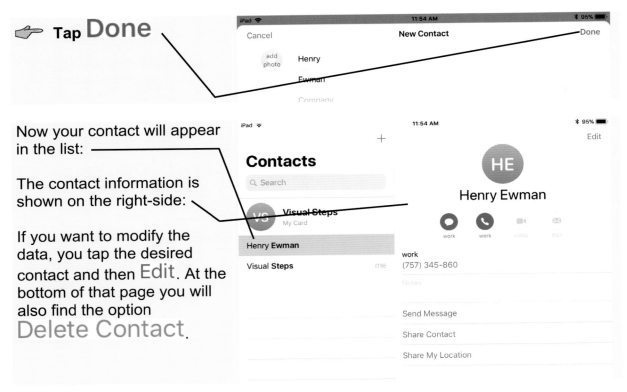

Now your contact will appear in the list:

The contact information is shown on the right-side:

If you want to modify the data, you tap the desired contact and then Edit. At the bottom of that page you will also find the option Delete Contact.

 Tip
Add a field for a middle name
A contact called De Vere will be listed under the letter D in the All Contacts list. If you prefer to classify this name under the letter V, you can add a field for the middle name:

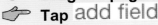 **Drag the page all the way upwards**
 Tap add field

- Continue on the next page -

You will see a list of fields you can add:

☞ **Tap** Middle name

The *Middle* field will be added. You can use this field for parts of a last name, such as 'de', 'le', 'la' or 'van'.

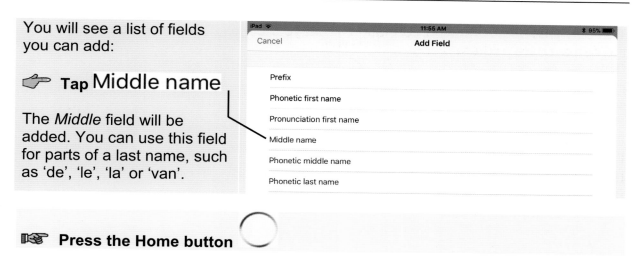

🖙 **Press the Home button** ◯

4.2 Calendar App

With the *Calendar* app you can keep track of your appointments, upcoming activities, birthdays and more. You open the *Calendar* app like this:

☞ **Tap** Calendar

When you open the *Calendar* app for the first time, you might see a window with the new options. You can close that window:

☞ **Tap** Continue

You may be asked whether you want to give permission for *Calendar* to access your location. For now this will not be necessary:

☞ **If necessary, tap** Don't Allow

The calendar opens showing the current date and time.

In the Day view you can select a different date here:

If you have selected a different date from the current date, you can use the Today button to quickly return to your current appointments:

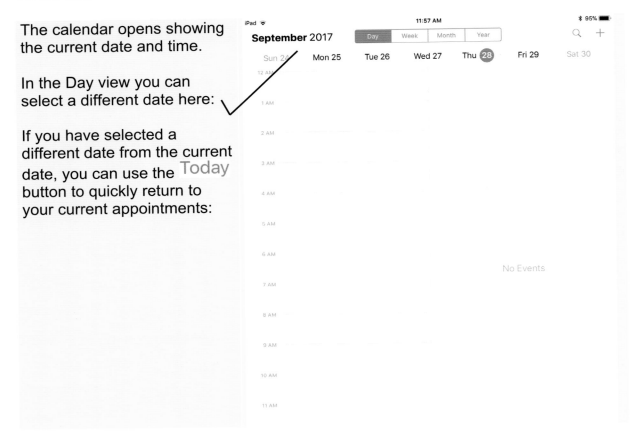

First, you check if the right calendar is displayed in the app:

☞ **Tap** Calendars

In this example you see several calendars. Depending on the accounts you have set up, for example, for *Hotmail*, you may also see other calendars.

This is how you select a calendar:

☞ **By** ON MY IPAD, **tap**
  • Calendar

☞ **Tap** Done

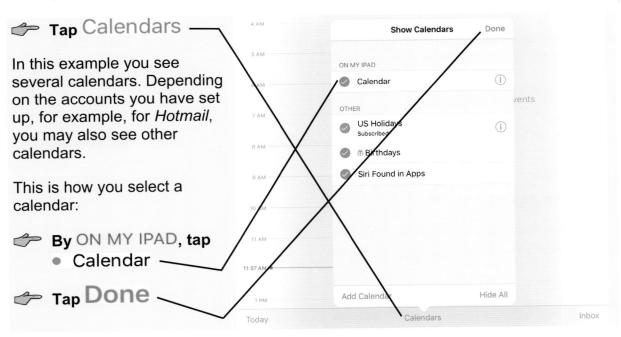

You can change the view to display the full week, month or year. This is how to view the full week:

☞ **Tap** Week

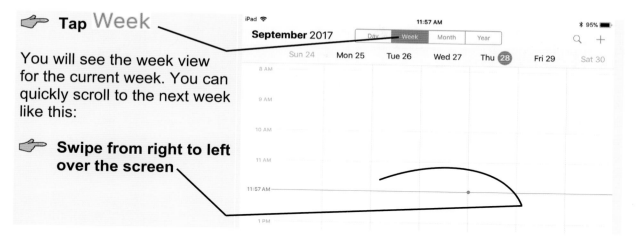

You will see the week view for the current week. You can quickly scroll to the next week like this:

☞ **Swipe from right to left over the screen**

In the *Calendar* app, an appointment is called an *event*. It is easy to add a new event to your calendar. Give it a try:

☞ **Tap** +

Now you can add a name and location for the event:

⌨ **Type a name, for example:** Tennis lessons

☞ **Tap** Location

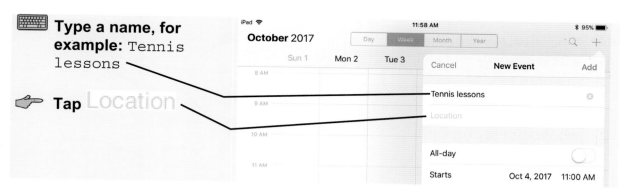

You may be asked if you want to give *Calendar* permission to use your location. For now this will not be necessary:

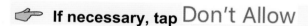

☞ **If necessary, tap** Don't Allow

Type a location, for instance: `Tennis court`

A search is made for locations and several options are shown. In this example, we will be using the general option, which is the text that you typed:

☞ **Tap** Tennis court

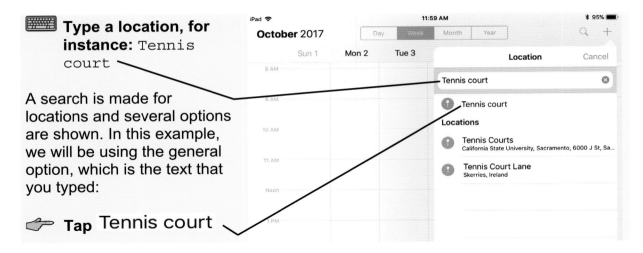

The date and time are displayed as four revolving wheels, a bit like a slot machine. You can change the time by turning the wheels. You need to touch the screen in a certain way:

☞ **Tap** Starts

☞ **Turn the wheel displaying the date to next Wednesday**

☞ **Turn the wheel displaying the hours to** 10

☞ **If necessary, turn the wheel displaying the minutes to** 00

☞ **If necessary, turn the wheel displaying the minutes to AM**

The end time will automatically be shifted to 11:00 a.m.:

If the event takes all day, tap by All-day:

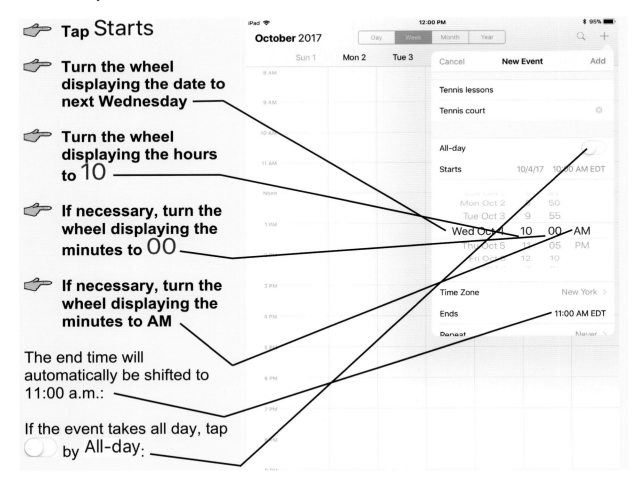

On the screen where you add an event, you will see some more options:

Repeat   Here you can set whether the event has to be repeated, and what the frequency is. For instance, every week or every month. By default, the Never option is selected.

Calendar   Select the calendar(s) in which the event needs to be recorded. You will see the event appear in the calendar, depending on which calendar(s) you display.

Invitees   Invite others to the event. Usually this is Busy. You will use an email address for that.

Travel Time Here you can add the travel time you need to get to the location for an event. Event alerts will take this time into account.

Alert   Here you can set up an alert, a sort of reminder, for a specific event. You can set a time for this alert: several minutes, hours, or days before the event. By default, the None option is selected.

Show As   The status of the event. Usually this is Busy.

After you have entered all the data, you add the event:

☞ **Tap Add**

The event is added to the calendar. To view the information on this event:

☞ **If necessary, drag across the calendar from right to left, until you see the event**

☞ **Tap the event**

To edit the event, you tap Edit. If you want to delete the event, you tap Delete Event.

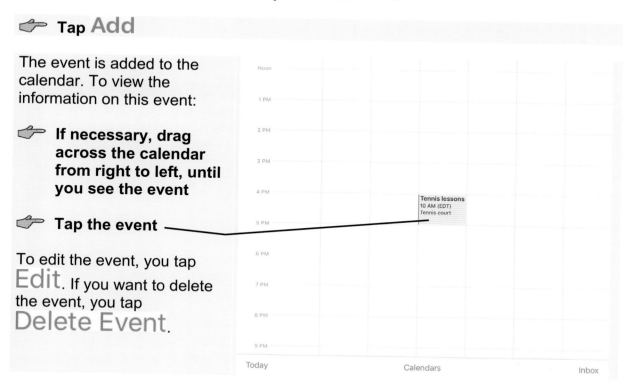

Tip

Add an event through the calendar
You can also add an event by pressing your finger to the calendar. Do this by pressing your finger on the desired date and time. Then you will see the *New Event* window, and you can enter the data.

☞ **Press the Home button**

4.3 Reminders App

The *Reminders* app will help you save important appointments and tasks. You can create lists of tasks yourself, including dates and locations.

☞ **Tap** Reminders

You will see an overview to which you can add a new task:

☞ **Tap the first line**

⌨ **Type a reminder**

On the keyboard:

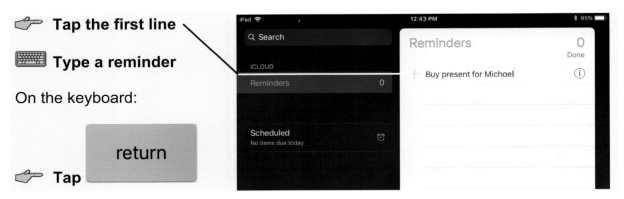

☞ **Tap** return

After you have added a reminder, you can add additional information:

👉 **Tap the reminder**

👉 **Tap** (i)

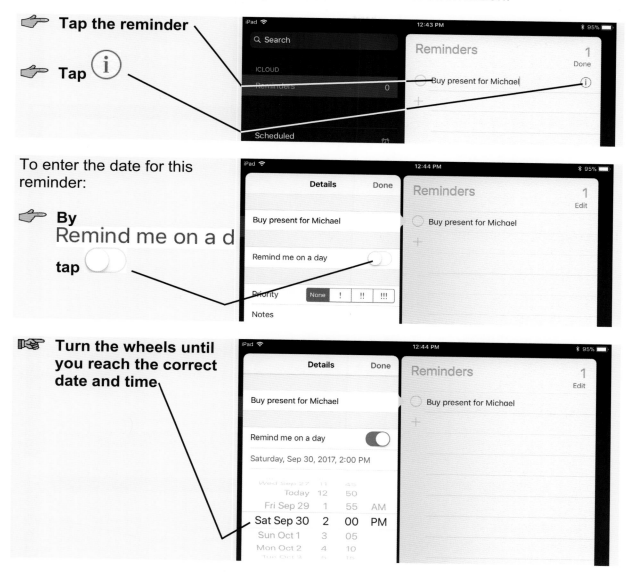

To enter the date for this reminder:

👉 **By**
Remind me on a d
tap ⬜

👉 **Turn the wheels until you reach the correct date and time**

You can add more information:

Repeat   Here you can set whether the event has to be repeated.

Priority   Here you can set up the importance of the event.

List   Select a list in which the reminder has to be saved. By **Add List** you can make new lists, for example if you want to separate work and private reminders.

Notes   Make an additional note for the reminder.

When you are done:

☞ Tap Done

You will see the reminder:

In order to complete the reminder, you tap the circle ◯ next to the reminder.

To delete the reminder:

☞ Tap Edit

☞ **By the reminder, tap** ⊖

☞ Tap Delete

☞ Tap Done

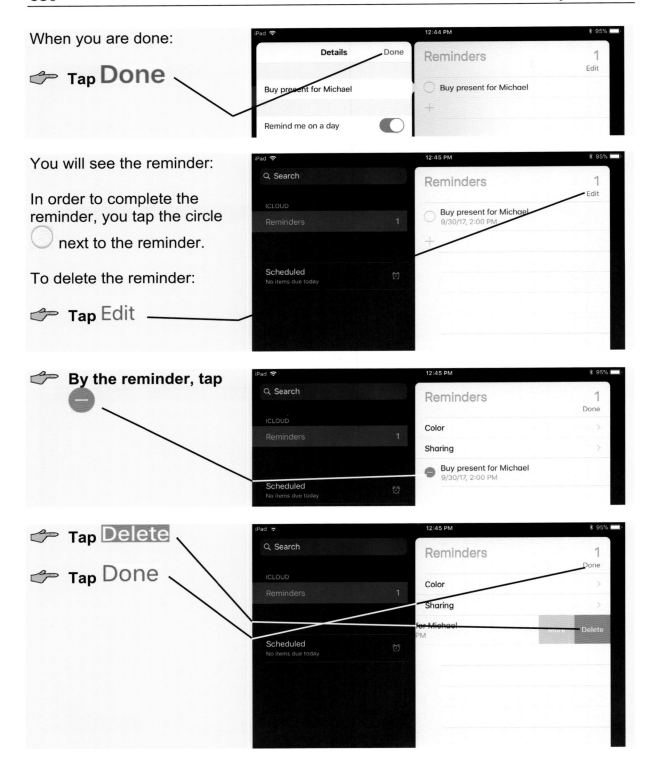

Tip

Sound the alarm

When the date and time of your reminder occurs, an alarm goes off and a small window pops up on your screen.

If the iPad is in sleep mode and you want to turn off the reminder:

 Swipe from left to right over the window

If the iPad is not in sleep mode you will see a message:

With **Remind** you can display the reminder again at a later point in time:

To mark as finished:

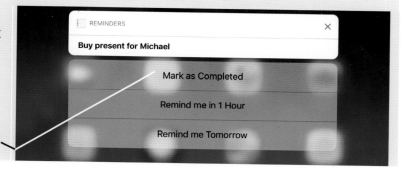

 Tap Mark as Completed

 Press the Home button

4.4 Maps App

With the *Maps* app you can search for a specific location and get directions for how to get there. This is how you open the *Maps* app:

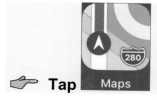

☞ **Tap** Maps

You will see the map of the country where you are located. You will be asked for permission to use your current location:

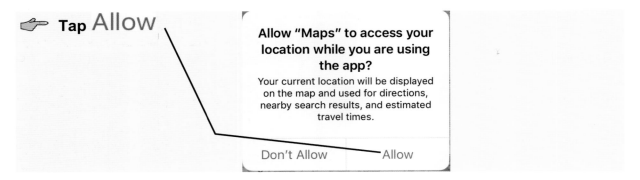

☞ **Tap** Allow

Allow "Maps" to access your location while you are using the app?

Your current location will be displayed on the map and used for directions, nearby search results, and estimated travel times.

Don't Allow   Allow

You might also see a window about helping to improve *Maps*. In this example, we will not choose to allow that:

☞ **Tap** Don't Allow

Now you can determine your current location:

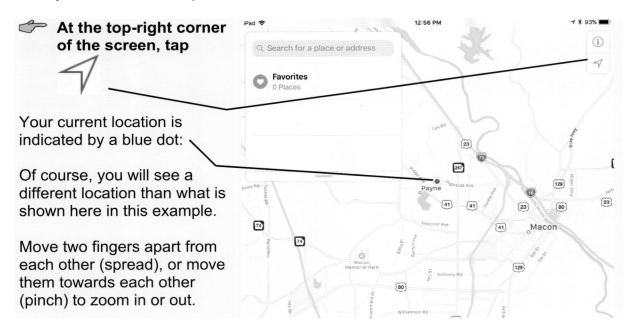

☞ **At the top-right corner of the screen, tap**

Your current location is indicated by a blue dot:

Of course, you will see a different location than what is shown here in this example.

Move two fingers apart from each other (spread), or move them towards each other (pinch) to zoom in or out.

You can use *Maps* to look for a specific location. You can search for a house or business address as well as a famous public place:

☞ **Tap the search box**

⌨ **Type:** Guggenheim

On the keyboard:

Search

☞ **Tap**

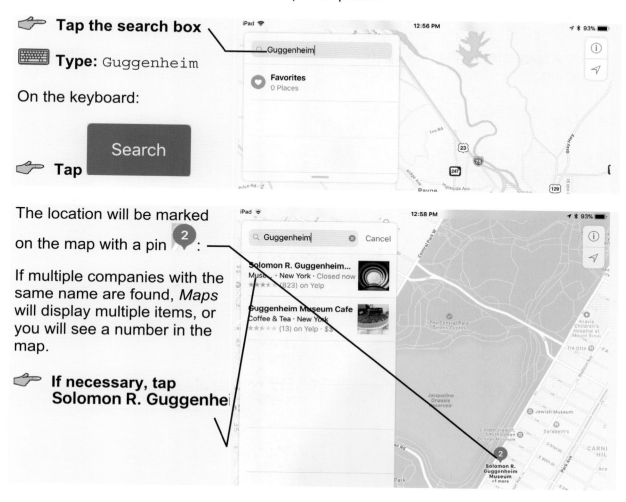

The location will be marked on the map with a pin **2** :

If multiple companies with the same name are found, *Maps* will display multiple items, or you will see a number in the map.

☞ **If necessary, tap Solomon R. Guggenhei**

Once you have found the desired location, you can plot a course for how to get there. This is how you do it:

☞ **Tap** **Directions**

Note that here you will find additional information on the location. If you swipe upwards across the screen you will see more options, such as adding the location to a contact.

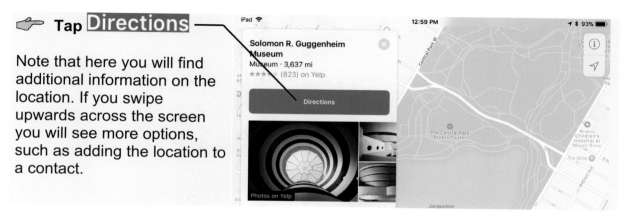

You may see a safety warning:

 **Tap** OK

The route is planned with your currect location as a starting point. You can change the starting point of your route as follows:

 **Tap** My Location

Here you will see the start and end point of the route. You are going to change the starting point: ────

By From:, **type:**
    Empire hotel ────

With ⇅ you can switch the start and end point: ────

To show the route by car:

 **Tap** Route ────

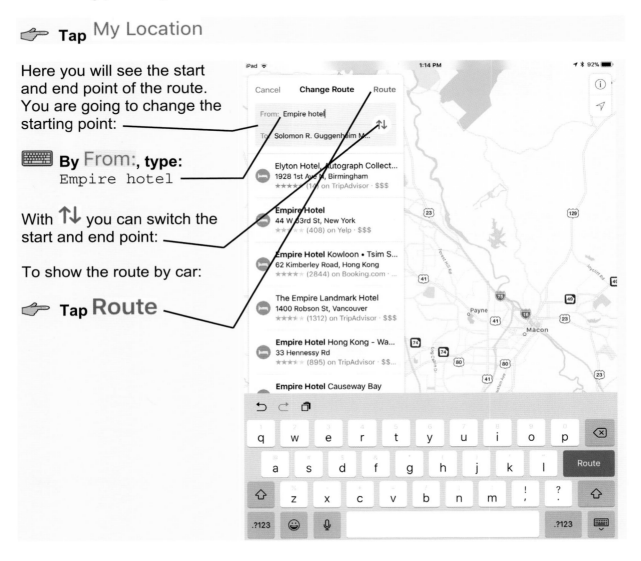

The car route will be shown starting from the starting point. The route is indicated by a blue line: ⎯⎯⎯⎯⎯

Here you can see the directions, the amount of time and mileage needed to take this route: ⎯⎯⎯⎯⎯

In this example an alternative route is also given, **18 min**:

You can also view the route

by **Walk** or **Transit**: ⎯⎯⎯⎯⎯

You can display the route step by step:

☞ **Tap** GO

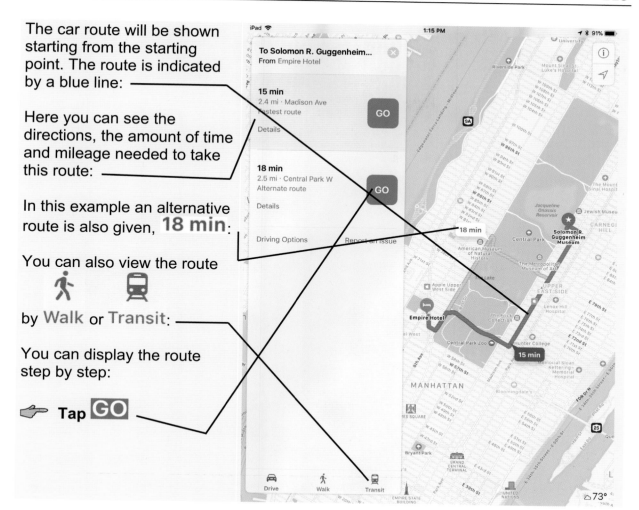

On an iPad with Wi-Fi you will see the first step of the route. You will also see the instruction in the box at the top:

In order to display the next step you need to swipe to the adjacent box:

☞ **Tap the box**

Now you can follow the route step by step by tapping the next box every time. For now this will not be necessary.

☞ **Tap** **End**

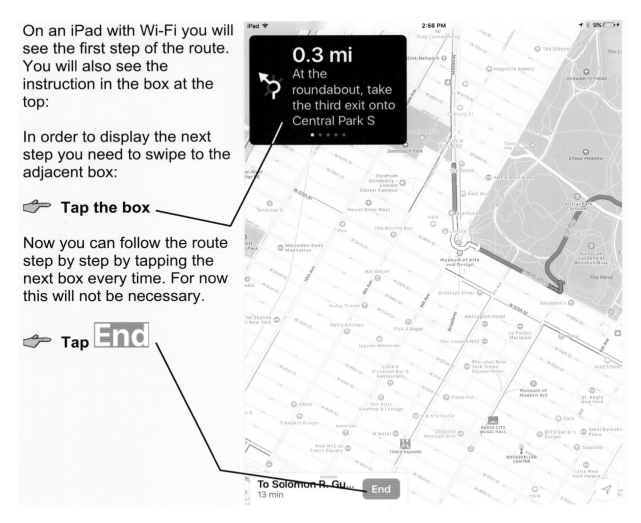

If you are using an iPad with Wi-Fi + 3G/4G and your own location has been entered as start point, the screen will look different. Because an iPad with 3G/4G is equipped with a built-in GPS receiver you can use it as a navigational device. You will hear the spoken instructions and you will see your current location marked on the screen. As soon as you move, the icon for your current location moves also and you will hear the next instruction. You will close the route:

☞ **Tap** **End**

☞ **Tap**

You will see your current location again.

Tip

Map view

With the (i) button in the top right-hand corner of the screen, you can see the settings for the view. You can choose between Map, Satellite or Transit. The Transit option displays information on the public transport. This view is not available for all the locations.

By default, also the current state of the traffic is indicated in the trip. If the line is orange or red, there will be delays. If you do not want to display this information, you tap Traffic in order to turn off the slider.

☞ **Press the Home button** ◯

4.5 Notes

Another standard app is the *Notes* app. You can use this app to take notes, but you can also add drawings or photos. In this section we will briefly discuss the various options:

👉 **Tap**

The first time you open this app, you will see information on the different functions:

👉 **Tap** Continue

You will create a new note:

👉 **Tap**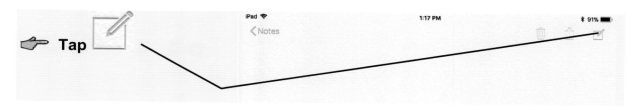

⌨ Type a short note

In the *Notes* app, you have the same text editing options as in the *Mail* app, for example.

You can also insert a table, format text, or make a list:

To draw:

👉 **Tap**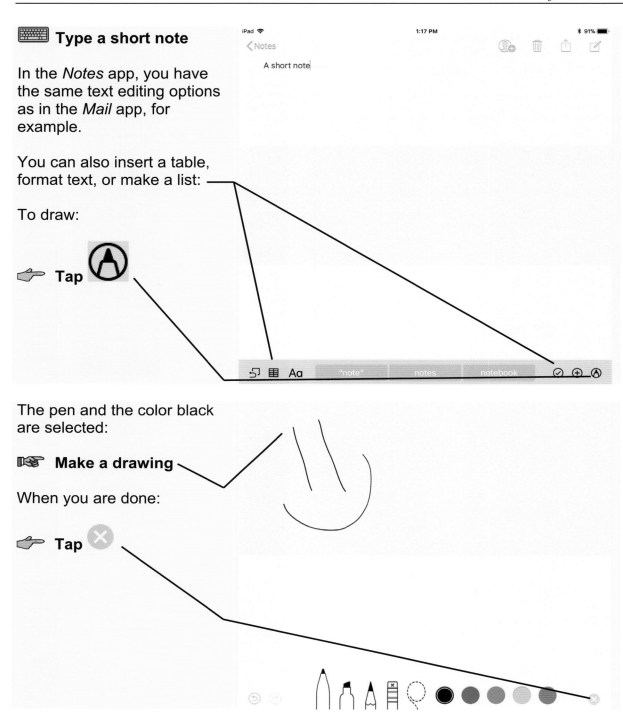

The pen and the color black are selected:

☞ **Make a drawing**

When you are done:

👉 **Tap**

There are more options available:

Share the note with others:

Delete the note:

Other options, such as printing:

With the ‹Notes button you can view all the other notes:

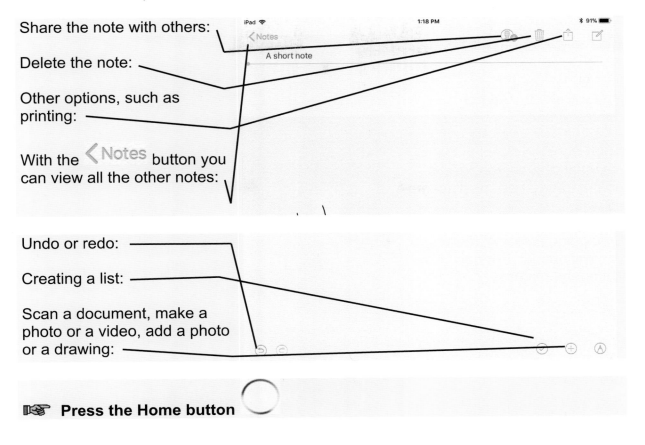

Undo or redo:

Creating a list:

Scan a document, make a photo or a video, add a photo or a drawing:

☞ **Press the Home button**

4.6 Searching on the iPad

The iPad has a search utility. This is how you open it:

👉 **Swipe downwards across the screen a bit, halfway the screen**

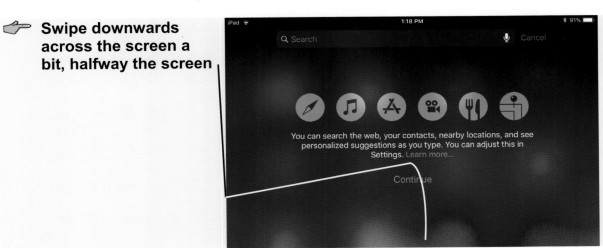

You can type your query right away. In this example we are searching for an event that has been previously entered in the *Calendar* app:

Type: Tennis
lessons

You will see the search
results at once:

Apart from the event in the
calendar, the search results
on the Internet are displayed
as well.

By tapping a search result
you will open it. For now this
will not be necessary.

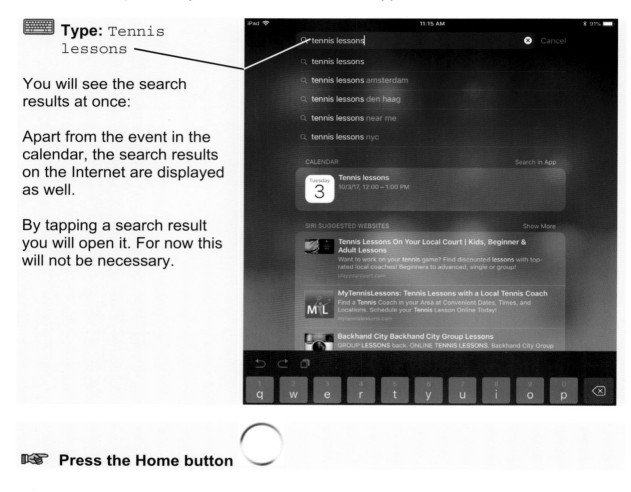

☞ **Press the Home button**

4.7 Siri

The iPad has a useful function with which you can give verbal instructions for the iPad to execute, and you can also use it to ask for information. This is how you open *Siri*:

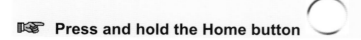

☞ **Press and hold the Home button**

Siri opens and you can ask a question out loud:

At the bottom of the screen:

 If necessary, tap

 Speak loudly and clearly and ask: What's the weather in New York?

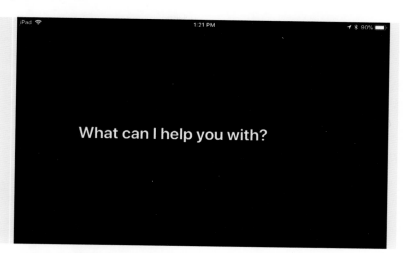

You will both see and hear the answer:

If you wish, you can tap the screen to open the weather forecast in the *Weather* app. For now this will not be necessary.

Pose another question:

 Tap

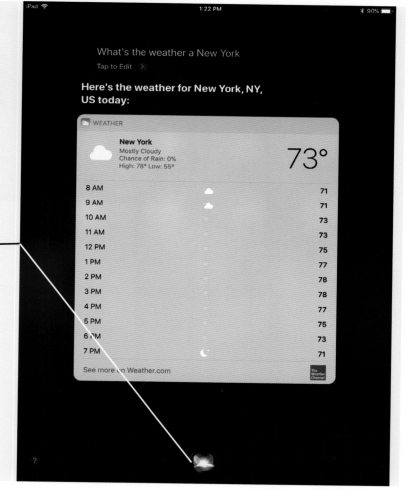

☞ Speak loudly and clearly and ask: Do I have any appointments today?

You will both see and hear the answer:

You can ask many more questions in the same way.

☞ Press the Home button

In this chapter you have learned more about some of the standard apps that are installed on your iPad.

4.8 Background Information

Dictionary

Calendar	An app that lets you keep track of your appointments and activities.
Contacts	An app that you can use to manage your contacts.
Event	An appointment in the *Calendar* app.
Field	Part of the information you can enter about a contact. For example, *First name* and *Postal code* are fields.
Flyover	In the *Maps* app you can view various urban areas and sights in 3D. This function is called *Flyover*.
Reminders	In the *Reminders* app you can save important appointments or tasks. You can create your own ToDo lists, including dates, locations, and reminders for things you should not forget.
Label	Name of a field.
Maps	An app where you can look for locations and addresses, view satellite photos and plan routes.
Notes	In the *Notes* app you can take notes, but also make a drawing, or add photos.
Siri	A function that lets you give verbal instructions for the iPad to execute, and lets you ask the iPad for information too.

Source: User Guide iPad, Wikipedia.

4.9 Tips

  Tip

Add an event from an email message

Mail recognizes dates in email messages and can insert them into your calendar. After a date has been recognized, you can quickly add an event to your calendar:

☞ **Tap the date**

☞ **Tap** Create Event

You will see the window in which you can enter the details of the event:

The subject of the email message is used as a name for the event:

After you have modified the data, you can add the event to your calendar:

☞ **Tap** Add

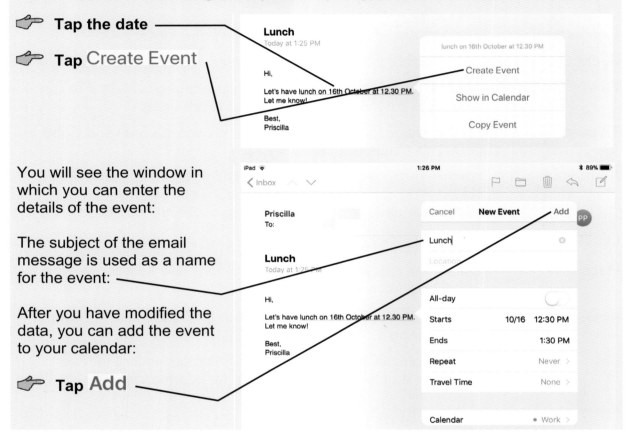

Tip

Add a photo
If you have a nice picture of your contact stored on your iPad, you can add this photo to his contact information. In *Chapter 6 Photos and Video* you can read how to take a picture with the iPad, and how to transfer photos to your iPad. This is to add an existing photo to your contact:

 Tap the desired contact
 **Tap** Edit

 Tap add photo

Tap Choose Photo

Select the photo album where the photo is stored:

Tap the desired album
Tap the desired photo

If you want, you can move the photo and adjust the scale by zooming in or out:

When you are ready:

 Tap Choose

The photo has been added to the contact data:

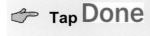 **Tap** Done

Tip

Flyover

In the *Maps* app you can view many urban areas and famous landmarks in 3D. This function is called *Flyover*.

Please note: This function is not available for some cities and well-known places.

In this example, you will be viewing the Golden Gate Bridge in San Francisco.

When you have found the location:

 Tap Flyover Tour

You will see the Golden Gate Bridge in 3D:

You can zoom in on the bridge and move the map around by dragging with your fingers. You can even rotate the image. It will appear as if you are flying right alongside the bridge.

 Press gently with your thumb and index finger and make a turning motion

In this way you can see an interesting object up close from all sides and discover new things about it.

To disable or turn off the 3D mode, tap the screen and ☒.

5. Downloading and Managing Apps

In the previous chapters you have become acquainted with the standard apps installed on the iPad. But there is so much more for you to discover! In the *App Store* you will find thousands of apps, free of charge or for a small fee, which you can download and install.

There are so many apps, it is impossible to list them all. Apps for news, magazines, the weather, games, recipes, sports results: you name it, there is bound to be an app available that interests you!

In this chapter you will learn how to download apps. If you want to download apps that charge a fee, you can pay for them safely with an *iTunes Gift Card*. This is a prepaid card available in a variety of different venues. You can also link a credit card to your *Apple ID*.

Once you have purchased apps, you can arrange them on your iPad in any order you want. You can also create folders that can hold multiple apps in the same folder. If you are no longer happy with a particular app, you can delete it.

In this chapter we will also explain how to use multiple apps at once. You can do this by switching between apps, or displaying multiple apps on the screen.

In this chapter you will learn how to:

- download and install a free app;
- use an *iTunes Gift Card*;
- move apps;
- save apps in a folder;
- delete apps;
- switch between recently used apps;
- simultaneously use multiple apps;
- close apps.

 Please note:

To follow the examples in this chapter you will need to have an *Apple ID*. If you have not created an *Apple ID* when you started using the iPad, you can still do that on the web page https://appleid.apple.com/account.

5.1 Downloading and Installing an App

In the *App Store* you will find thousands of apps that can be used on your iPad. This is how you open the *App Store*:

☞ **If necessary, wake the iPad up from sleep mode or turn it on** 👣²

☞ **Tap** App Store

The first time you log in to the *App Store*, you might see a window about using your location. In this example, this is not allowed:

☞ **If necessary, tap** Don't Allow

You will see the **Today** page, where attention is paid to a number of new and popular apps. You will open the *Apps* page:

☞ **Tap** ☰ Apps

All kinds of apps are displayed on this page:

Just scroll through the page. In many sections you can drag upwards and downwards, but also to the left and to the right.

You will also see lists with new apps, free apps, paid apps, and categories.

In this example you will use the search function to find an app:

☞ **Tap** 🔍 Search

👉 **Tap the search box**

⌨️ **Type:** weather channel

On the keyboard:

Search

👉 **Tap**

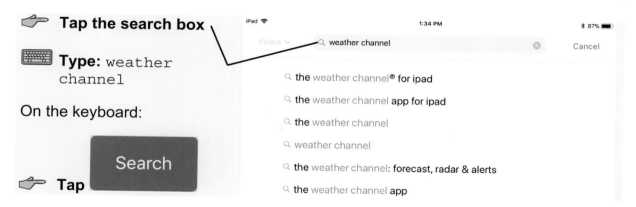

You see the search results. Just take a look at the information on this app:

👉 **Tap**

More information and reviews about the app are shown. This is how you download an app:

👉 **Tap** **GET**

You may need to sign in with your *Apple ID* in order to install the app:

👉 **If necessary, tap** Use Existing Apple ID

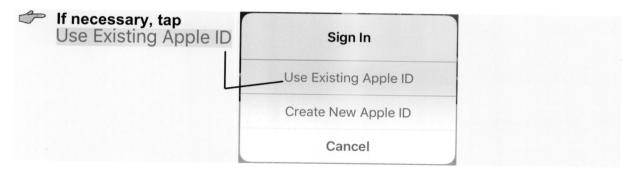

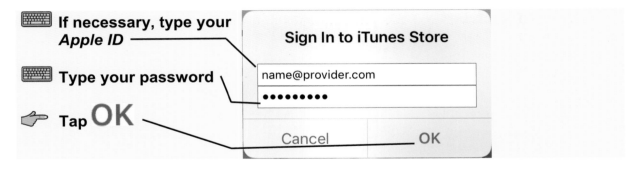

If necessary, type your *Apple ID*

Type your password

Tap OK

⇨ Please note:

If you have not downloaded an app in the *App Store* before, you will possibly see a message. Your *Apple ID* needs to be completed with extra data, such as your country, address information, and a payment method for paid apps. If you want to install a free app, as in this example, you can select **None**. You also need to agree to the general terms and conditions. Follow the instructions on the screens in order to go through the procedure.

You will see a new window:

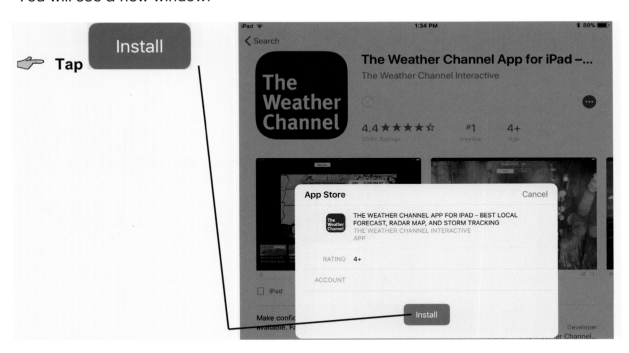

☞ Tap **Install**

You might need to fill in your *Apple ID* again:

☞ **If necessary, sign in with your *Apple ID*** 7

You may see a window where you are asked if you always want to enter a password when you install an app, or if you only want to do this after 15 minutes have passed after you were last signed in. We recommend always entering a password, especially if you add a credit to your *Apple ID*. In such a case, you can prevent others from using your credit to purchase items in the store.

👉 **If necessary, tap the desired option**

The app will be installed. It is ready when you see the **OPEN** button. For now you do not need to open the app, you can take a look at it later on, in your own time.

👉 **Press the Home button** ◯

You will see the app at the second page:

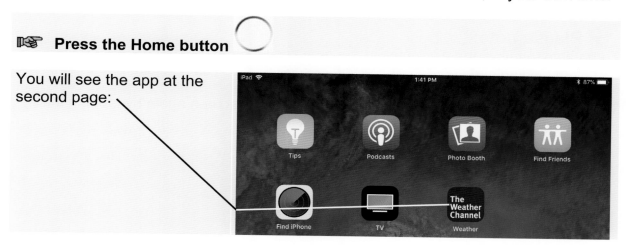

💡 **Tip**

Manage apps
In *section 5.3 Moving Apps* you can read how to move apps on a page, and between pages.

In the next sections you will learn how to link an *iTunes Gift Card* to your *Apple ID*, with which you can purchase apps, if you wish.

5.2 Redeem an iTunes Gift Card

The *App Store* offers various payment methods. One of these is the *iTunes Gift Card*. This is a prepaid card that you can use to purchase items in the *App Store.* By using an *iTunes Gift Card*, you can avoid using a credit card. In this section you will read how to redeem your credit.

The *iTunes Gift Card* comes in different denominations. You can purchase these cards from the *Apple Online Store*, at your *Apple* retailer and at thousands of other retailers across the USA, the UK and Australia.

You can also get the *iTunes Gift Card* at www.instantitunescodes.com. This web store allows you to pay online and you will receive the code for the card by email, right away. *iTunes Gift Cards* purchased at this store are only valid in the United States.

 Please note:
To be able to follow the examples in the next section, you need to have an *iTunes Gift Card* available. If you do not (yet) have such a card, you can just read the text.

The *App Store* is still opened and you can display the screen again by tapping the icon on the Dock:

☞ **Tap**

You are going to redeem the credit on the *iTunes Gift Card*. At the top of the page:

☞ **Tap**   Apps

You will see a window with information and options for your *Apple ID*:

☞ **Tap**
Redeem Gift Card or C

You need to sign in with your *Apple ID* again:

☞ **If necessary, sign in with your *Apple ID* 👓7**

Now you will see a window where you can enter the code for your *iTunes Gift Card*.

You will find the code under the scratch layer on the back of the card: ———

☞ **Carefully remove the scratch layer**

Now you will see a code composed of 16 digits and letters that you need to enter. You can use the camera of the iPad or just type the code:

☞ **Tap the desired method**

☞ **Follow the instructions onscreen**

When the code is approved, you will see a confirmation and the balance of your credit.

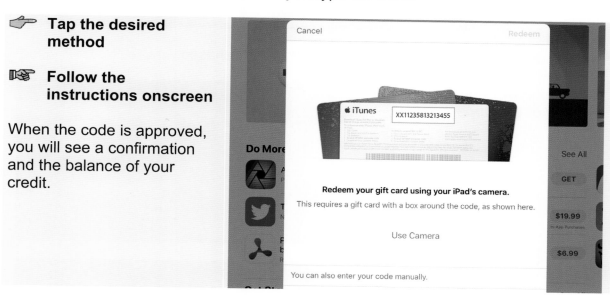

Now you have added credit to your *Apple ID*, you can purchase apps in the *App Store*. This works the same way as downloading and installing a free app. With a paid app, you will see the price $2.99 instead of GET .
In order to execute the operations in this book you will not need to install a paid app.

☞ **Press the Home button**

5.3 Moving Apps

You can completely adjust the order of the apps on your iPad to your own taste, by moving the apps around.

Possibly your screen will display the home screen. This is how you scroll to the second page with the apps you just bought:

☞ **Swipe across the screen from right to left**

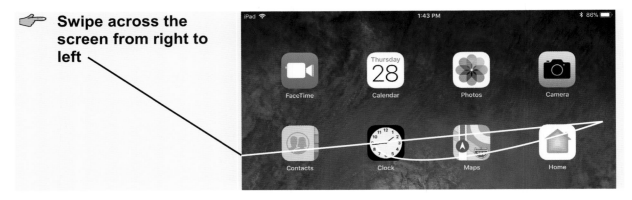

Now you will see the page with the apps you have purchased:

☞ **Press your finger on one of the apps**

The apps will start to jiggle, a little cross ⊠ will appear, and now you can move them:

Drag Weather **to the right side of the other app**

Now the apps have changed place. You can also move an app to a different page. This is how you move an app to the home screen:

Drag Weather **against the left border of the screen**

When you see the home screen:

Release Weather

Now the app has been placed between the other apps on the home screen:

Of course, you can also change the order of the apps on this page. For now, this will not be necessary.

5.4 Storing Apps in Folders

You can also store related apps in a separate folder. Here is how to do that:

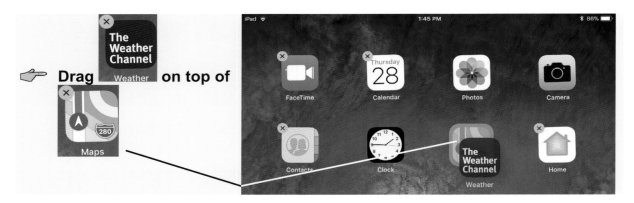

☞ **Drag** Weather **on top of**

A suitable name will be suggested for the new folder. If you want you can also change this name:

☞ **Tap the name** —————

⌨ **Type:** Weather and traffic

If you are satisfied with the name:

☞ **Tap next to the folder**

> Weather and traffic ⊗

Now you will see this folder on the home screen:

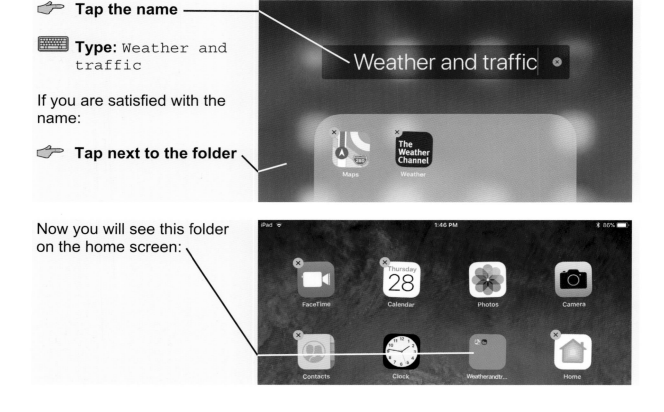

This is how to stop the apps from jiggling:

 **Press the Home button**

Now the apps have stopped moving. To view the contents of the folder:

 **Tap** Weatherandtr...

This is how you remove the app from the folder again:

👉 **Press your finger on one of the apps**

👉 **Drag the app from the folder**

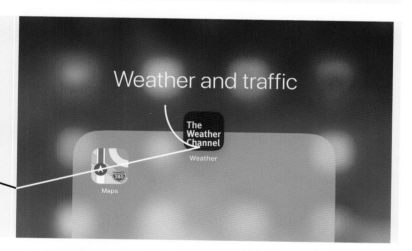

Now the app has returned to the home screen:

If you remove the other app from the folder too, the folder will disappear.

👉 **Drag the other app from the folder** 👣⁸

You stop the apps from jiggling:

☞ **Press the Home button**

5.5 Deleting an App

Have you downloaded an app that turns out to be a bit disappointing? You can easily delete such an app.

☞ **Press your finger on one of the apps**

☞ **By the app you want to delete, tap** ⊗

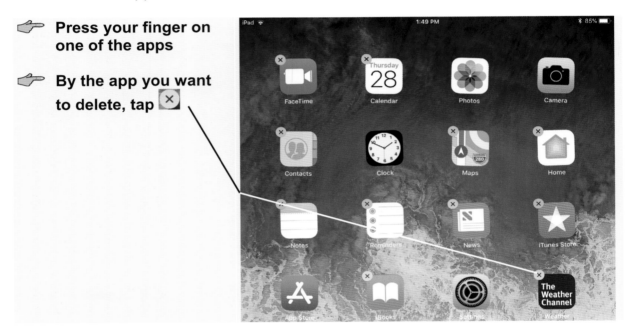

If you really want to delete the app:

☞ **Tap** Delete

> **Delete " Weather "?**
> Deleting this app will also delete its data.
>
> Cancel   Delete

The app will be deleted. Stop the apps from jiggling again:

☞ **Press the Home button**

5.6 Switching Between Recently Used Apps

By using the Home button, you can quickly switch between the apps you have recently used. Just try it:

🖝 **Press the Home button twice quickly**

You will see the recently used apps in the app switcher:

You will switch to the *Contacts* app:

👉 **Tap** **Contacts**

 Tip

Multiple open apps

If you have opened more than four apps you will not see them on your screen all at once. You can swipe across the screen from left to right or in the opposite direction to see the other opened apps.

You will see the *Contacts* app. You can also use the Dock to switch between apps:

☞ **Drag across the screen from bottom to top**

You will see the Dock with the three apps that were used last:

Switch to the *Maps* app:

☞ **Tap**

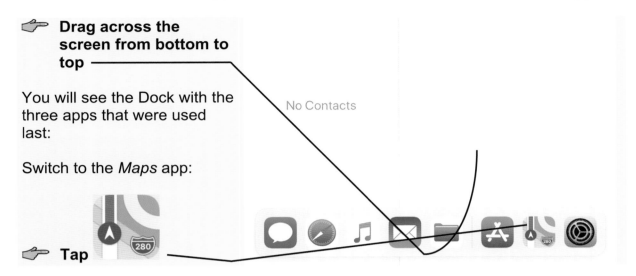

5.7 Using Multiple Apps At Once

You can open and use two apps at the same time. To get the best view you can hold the iPad in horizontal position:

☞ **Turn the iPad to the right or left towards a horizontal position**

The *Maps* app is opened and you will also open the *Mail* app. The first option is to open the app as a small second window, and display it on top of the current app. This is also called the *Slide Over* option.

☞ **Drag across the screen from bottom to top**

You will see the Dock again:

☞ **Drag** [mail icon] **to the right-hand side of the screen (but not completely to the side)**

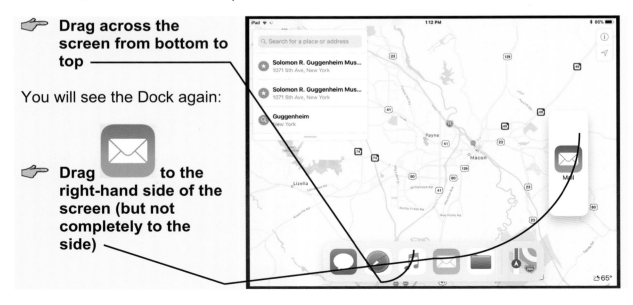

You can work in *Mail* just as you are used to. A second option is to split the screen in two halves. This is called *Split View*. You can switch from the Slide Over view to the Split View:

👉 **Drag** ⬤ **in the window a bit to the bottom right-hand side**

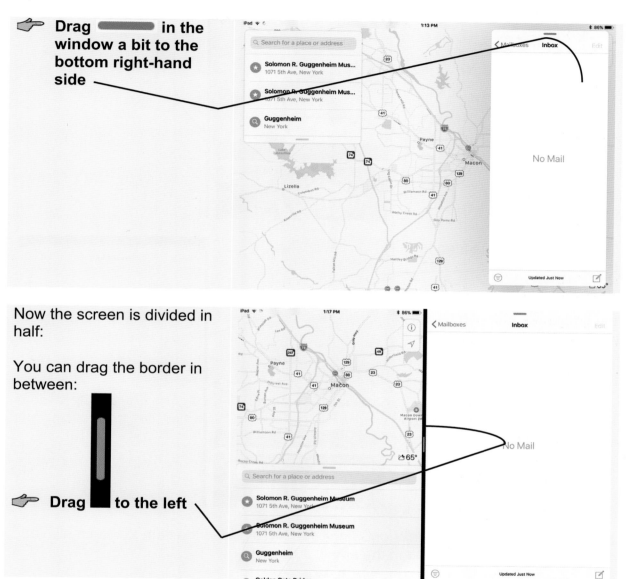

Now the screen is divided in half:

You can drag the border in between:

👉 **Drag** ▌ **to the left**

A useful option is dragging the content from one window to another. In this example you insert the location into an email. In the same way, you could add a photo, calendar item, or contact.

☞ **Open a new email** 👣4

☞ **Drag** [____] **to
the *Mail* window**

The item has been added to
the email: ——————

To go back to a single app in
the screen:

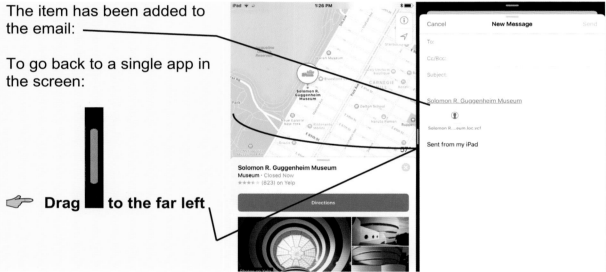

☞ **Drag** ▮ **to the far left**

Now you will only see the *Mail* app. Since you have added the item to the email, you
can also open it directly through the email. Just try it:

☞ **Send the email to
yourself** 👣9

Once you have received the email again, you open it:

☞ **Open the email** 𝄞⁵

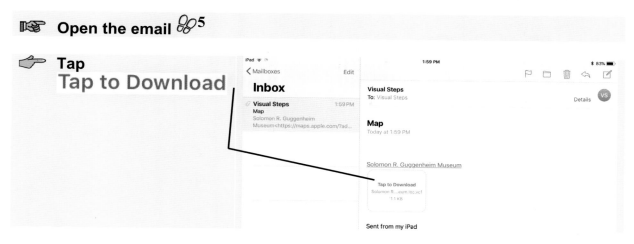

A small window with information from *Maps* is opened, and from here you can display the location:

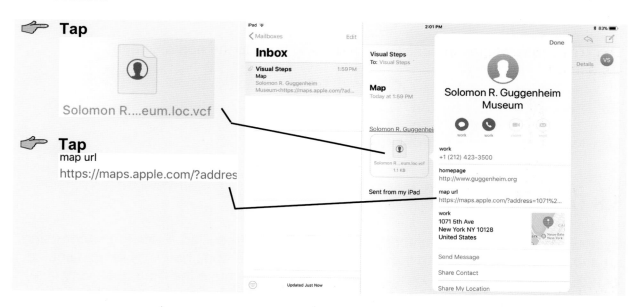

You will see the location in the *Maps* app. Now you want to go back to the email message. You do this with a button in the top left-hand corner of the screen:

The *Mail* app is displayed again. You are going back to the home screen:

☞ **Press the Home button**

☞ **Rotate the iPad a quarter turn**

5.8 Disabling Apps

By now, you have used a number of different apps on the iPad. Each time after using an app, you have returned to the home screen. But the apps have not been disabled by this action. Actually, this is not really necessary, because the iPad uses very little power in sleep mode, and you have the advantage of being able to continue at the same spot, once you start working again.

Nevertheless, it is possible to close the apps, if you want. This is how you do it:

☞ **Press the Home button twice**

You will see the recently used apps:

To close an app:

☞ **Drag the app window upwards** ──────

The app will be closed.

You can close the other apps in the same way:

☞ **Close the other apps too**

☞ **Press the Home button** ◯

In this chapter you have learned how to download an app from the *App Store*. You have also seen how you can manage and arrange your apps on the screen, and how you work with multiple apps at once.

There are more apps in which you can download files, both paid and free. You can download eBooks, podcasts, and music, for example. In the *Tips* at the back of this chapter you can read more on this subject.

5.9 Background Information

Dictionary

App Store	Online store where you can buy and download apps. You can also download many apps for free.
Apple ID	Combination of an email address and a password, also called *iTunes App Store Account*. You need to have an *Apple ID* in order to download apps from the *App Store*.
E-reader	A device with which you can read digital books. With the *iBooks* app you can turn your iPad into an e-reader.
iBooks	An app that lets you read digital books (eBooks).
iBookstore	A bookstore that goes with the *iBooks* app. Here you can download lots of books, free and at a price.
iTunes	A program that lets you manage the content of your iPad on your pc. But you can also use *iTunes* to listen to music files, watch movies, and import CDs. In *iTunes* you will also find the *iTunes Store* and the *App Store*.
iTunes Gift Card	A prepaid card that can be used to purchase items in the *App Store.*
iTunes Store	Online store where you can download and purchase music, movies, tv shows, podcasts, audio books and more.
Library	In *Music*: an overview of all the songs you have stored on your iPad. In *iBooks*: a book case containing all the books you have purchased and downloaded.
Multitasking gesture	Touch gestures with four or five fingers at once, with which you display the multitasking bar, switch between opened apps, or go back to the home screen.
Music	An app that plays music.
Playlist	A collection of songs, ordered in a certain way.

- Continue on the next page -

Podcast An episodic program, delivered through the Internet. Podcast episodes can be audio or video files and can be downloaded with the *iTunes Store*.

Slide over With this option you can open and use two apps at the same time. The second app is shown in a small window on top.

Split View With this option you can use two apps at the same time.

Source: User Guide iPad.

5.10 Tips

 Tip

Update apps
After a while, the apps you have installed on your iPad will be updated for free. These updates may be necessary in order to solve existing problems. But an update may also add new functionalities, such as a new game level. Although the apps are usually automatically updated, it is useful to check whether all the apps are really up-to-date, every once in a while. To do this, you open the *App Store*:

☞ **Open the *App Store* ⸖10**

☞ **Tap**

The program will search for available updates for your apps. If there are any updates available, you tap **UPDATE** by the app. Or you tap Update All, if you want to update all the apps.

 Tip

Download a paid app once again
If you have deleted a paid app, you will be able to download it again, free of charge. Although you need to use the same *Apple ID* as the first time.

☞ **Open the *App Store* ⸖10**

☞ **Tap**

☞ **Tap** Purchased

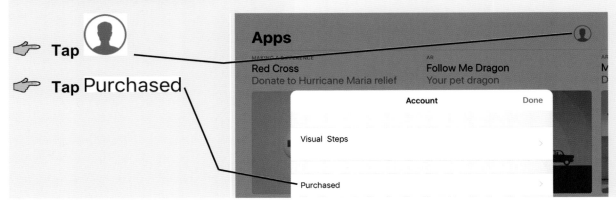

- Continue on the next page -
You will see the apps you have previously downloaded:

If you want to download the app again, you tap 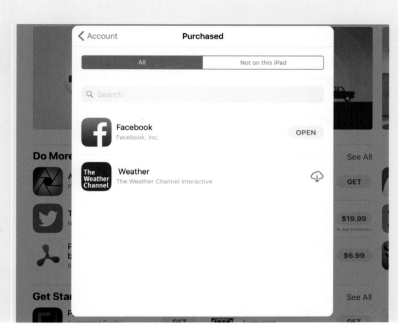. If this was a paid app, you will not be charged if you download this app for a second time.

In the *App Store* you will also see the symbol by the apps you have recently downloaded.

Tip
Signing out in the App Store
It is wise to sign out in the *App Store*, especially if you have a credit, or have linked your credit card to your *Apple ID*. Even if you have selected the setting to enter a password if more than 15 minutes have passed since signing in, you should still sign out every time. If others are allowed to use your iPad as well, this will prevent them from purchasing things with your credit, or using your credit card. Keep in mind that many games contain in-app purchasing options that require an *Apple ID*.

☞ **Tap**

☞ **Tap** Sign Out

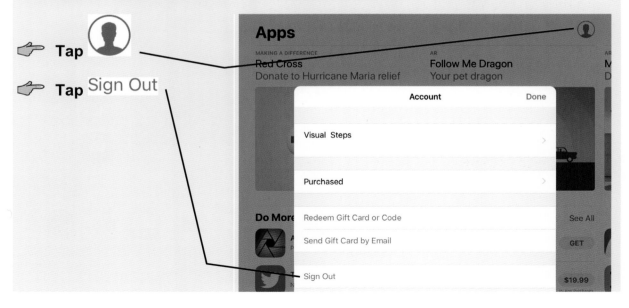

💡 Tip

Multitasking gestures

The iPad will also react to gestures made with four or five fingers at once. These are called *multitasking gestures*. First, you need to check if the multitasking gestures have been enabled on your iPad:

☞ **Open the *Settings* app**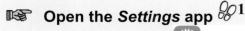

☞ **If necessary, tap** 🔘 General

☞ **If necessary, tap** Multitasking

☞ **If necessary, drag the slider** ⬜ **by** Gestures **to the right**

There are three different multitasking gestures:

☞ **Swipe upwards across the screen, with four or five fingers**

The *Control Center* and app switcher are shown.
This is how you make it disappear:

☞ **Press the Home button** ⬜

You can also quickly switch between opened apps without using the multitasking bar:

 Swipe across the screen from right to left, with four or five fingers

You will see the next opened app.

 Swipe across the screen from left to right, with four or five fingers

You will see the previous opened app.

The last multitasking gesture will quickly take you back to the home screen, without using the Home button:

 Use your thumb and three or four finger to make a pinching gesture on the screen

Now you will see the home screen.

 Tip

The Music app

Your iPad is equipped with an extensive music player, the *Music* app. If you have stored any music files on your computer, you can transfer this music to your iPad, through *iTunes*. In the *iTunes Store* you can also purchase songs or entire albums. Apart from that, the app has an option to subscribe to *Apple Music*, a music service that offers you unlimited access to music, at a fee. You can use this music service for a month, without being charged, but you need to enter your credit card data.

The *Music* app is not extensively discussed in this book. In this example we assume that there are already some music files stored on the iPad, or that an *Apple Music* subscription has been activated. We will only discuss the playback options.

 **Open the *Music* app** $\%^{11}$

- Continue on the next page -

At the bottom of the screen you see the various components of the *Music* app:

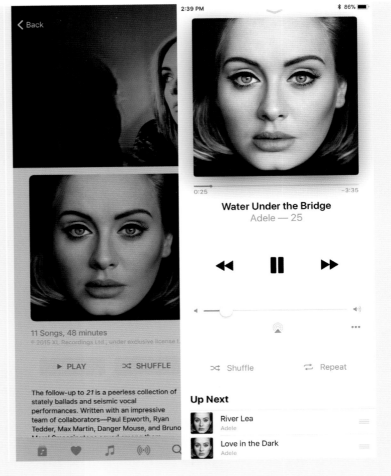

📑 Library: Recently added music.

♥ For You: For you with suggestions for music that suits you.

🎵 Browse: Browse and discover new music.

((•)) Radio: Listen to the radio.

🔍 Search: Search music.

Through the *Library* on the 📑 Library page you navigate to the artists, songs, albums, or playlists:

This is how all the buttons work:

	Go back to the overview of all the songs in the *Library*.
0:11	Drag the playback bar ⎯⎯● to go to a specific place in the song.
♥	With this option you can 'like' a song.
◀◀	This button has multiple functions: • tap once: skip to the beginning of the current song. • tap twice: skip to the previous song. • press and hold your finger gently on the button to fast backward.
▶▶	This button has multiple functions: • tap once: skip to the next song. • press and hold your finger gently on the button to fast forward.
	Pause.

- Continue on the next page

▶ Play, or resume play.

View the songs on the album (if these songs are stored on your iPad).

Volume control.

⤭ **Shuffle** Shuffle: play in random order.

⇄ **Repeat** Repeat, there are three options:

- ↰ : do not use repeat.

- ⇄ : all songs will be repeated.

- ⇄¹ : the current song will be repeated.

Add song to playlist, show in *iTunes Store* or delete song.

If you scroll upwards across the screen, you will see the control buttons appear in the *Control Center*:

While you are listening to music, you can also use other apps.

Nowadays, lots of people use the *Spotify* music service. You can download an app for this service on the iPad. *Spotify* can be used for free if you do not mind the commercials. If you prefer not to hear commercials interfering with your music, you can sign up for a paid subscription.

Tip

Podcast

You can use the *Podcast* app to search for podcasts. Podcasts are episodes of a program available on the Internet. There are thousands of podcasts available. These can be anything from a recorded broadcast of a particular radio program, lecture, live musical performance, and many other types of events. You can download a podcast like this:

☞ **Browse to the second page** 🦶**14**

☞ **Open the *Podcast* app** 🦶**15**

At the bottom of the screen:

☞ **Tap** 🔘 Browse

▶ Listen Now   ▦ Library   🔘 Browse   🔍 Search

You will see a page with many different podcasts. You can see more information by tapping an individual podcast:

👉 **Tap a podcast**

To download an episode:

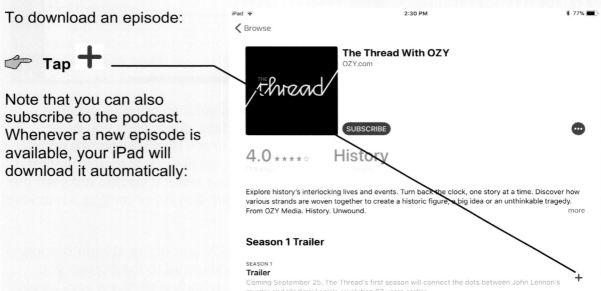

👉 **Tap** ➕

Note that you can also subscribe to the podcast. Whenever a new episode is available, your iPad will download it automatically:

iPad 📶   2:30 PM   ✳ 77% 🔋
‹ Browse

The Thread With OZY
OZY.com

thread

SUBSCRIBE   ⋯

4.0 ★★★★☆   History

Explore history's interlocking lives and events. Turn back the clock, one story at a time. Discover how various strands are woven together to create a historic figure, a big idea or an unthinkable tragedy. From OZY Media. History. Unwound.   more

Season 1 Trailer

SEASON 1
Trailer
Coming September 25. The Thread's first season will connect the dots between John Lennon's murder and Vladimir Lenin's revolution 63 years earlier.   +

When the download is completed, you can view the podcast by tapping 🗄 Library. To play an episode you need to tap the podcast first to see the episodes you have downloaded. Then you can play it by clicking it.

6. Photos and Video

The iPad is equipped with two cameras that will give you plenty of opportunity for taking pictures or shooting videos. The *Camera* app lets you use the built-in back camera of the iPad, so you can take a picture or make a video of an interesting object. While taking a picture, you can focus, zoom in and zoom out. If you switch to the front camera of the iPad, you can also take a self-portrait (selfie).

To view the pictures and videos on your iPad, you can use the *Photos* app. You can also edit the pictures in several ways.

You do not need to limit yourself and only use the photos you have made with the iPad. In this chapter you can read how to transfer photos from your computer to the iPad. Of course, you can also do it the other way round and transfer the photos you have made with the iPad to your computer.

In this chapter you will learn how to:

- take pictures with your iPad;
- focus on an object;
- zoom in and zoom out;
- shoot a video with your iPad;
- view photos;
- play a video recording;
- copy photos and video to the computer;
- copy photos and video to your iPad;
- automatically enhance photos;
- crop a photo;
- find the other options for pictures.

6.1 Taking Pictures

You can use the *Camera* app to take pictures. This is how to open the app:

☞ **If necessary, wake the iPad up from sleep or turn it on** ✎²

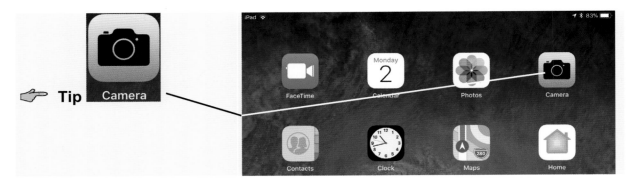

☞ **Tip** Camera

When the app is opened, you might see a message asking you if the current location can be used. This information is used to indicate the location of where the picture will be taken:

You can change the settings and turn on the location services for the camera.

☞ **Tap** Allow

Now you will see the image that is recorded by the camera on the back of the iPad.

☞ **Point the camera towards the object you want to photograph**

↳ **Please note:**
Make sure there is enough light. Your iPad is not equipped with flash photography. If you take a picture in poor lighting conditions, the photo will look grainy and out of focus.

This is how you take a picture:

☞ **Tap** ⬤ —————————

The photo will be stored on your iPad.

Before you take a picture, you can focus on a specific area:

☞ **Tap the part of the object you want to focus on** ———

The exposure will be adjusted to the selected object. If you tap a dark part of the object, you will see the image become lighter.

Is the image too light? Then you need to tap a lighter part of the object.

Take another picture:

☞ **Tap** ⬤ —————————

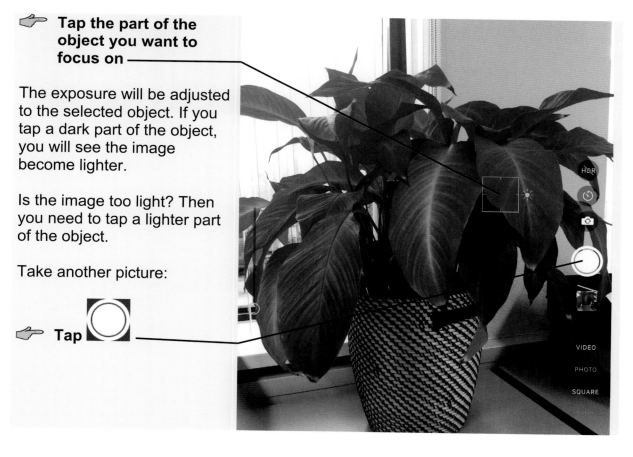

With the digital zoom you can zoom in on an object, up to five times. You can only do this by using the camera on the back of the iPad. This is how you zoom in:

☞ **Move your thumb and index finger apart, on the screen**

You will zoom in on the object. Take another picture:

☞ **Tap** ⭕

This is how you zoom out again:

☞ **Drag the slider** down

Or:

☞ **Move your thumb and index finger towards each other, on the screen**

Tip

Taking square pictures or panorama pictures
Now you have taken picture with the usual ratio. But you can also take square pictures, or panoramic pictures. In order to do this, you drag PHOTO upwards until the desired option is selected. If you want to take a panoramic picture, you need to move the iPad in one smooth movement to the right or to the left.

6.2 Shooting Videos

You can also use the back camera of the iPad for shooting videos:

 Tip

Turn sideways
Do you intend to play your video on a TV or on a larger screen? Then position your iPad sideways, in landscape mode. This way, your image will fill the entire screen.

☞ **If desired, turn your iPad a quarter turn, so it is in the horizontal position**

👉 **Swipe** VIDEO
downwards ——————

VIDEO turns into VIDEO:

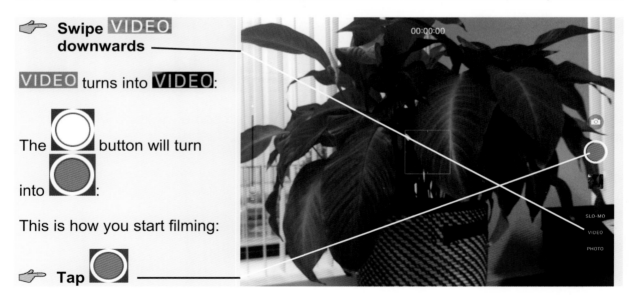

The ⬤ button will turn

into ⬤:

This is how you start filming:

👉 **Tap** ⬤ ——————

While you are shooting the film, the button will turn into ⬤. This is how you stop filming:

👉 **Tap**

You can reset the *Camera* app for taking pictures:

☞ **Swipe**  **upwards**

☞ **If desired, turn the iPad a quarter turn until it is in upright position again**

☞ **Press the Home button** ⬤

6.3 Viewing Photos

You have taken a number of pictures with your iPad. You can view these photos with the *Photos* app. This is how you open the app:

☞ **Tap**

If you open the *Photos* app for the first time, you will see some windows with information:

☞ **Tap** Continue

In the next window:

☞ **If necessary, tap** *Not now*

♀ **Tip**
Transfer photos to the iPad with iTunes
You can also use *iTunes* to transfer photos taken with your digital camera to your iPad. Very handy, if you want to show your favorite pictures to others. In *section 6.6 Copying Photos and Videos to Your iPad Through iTunes* you can read how to do this.

You will see miniatures of the photos you took:

You will see the collections of your pictures, grouped by location and recording date:

You will also see a video among the photos:

You are going to the screen where the albums have been arranged in a more orderly way:

👉 **Tap**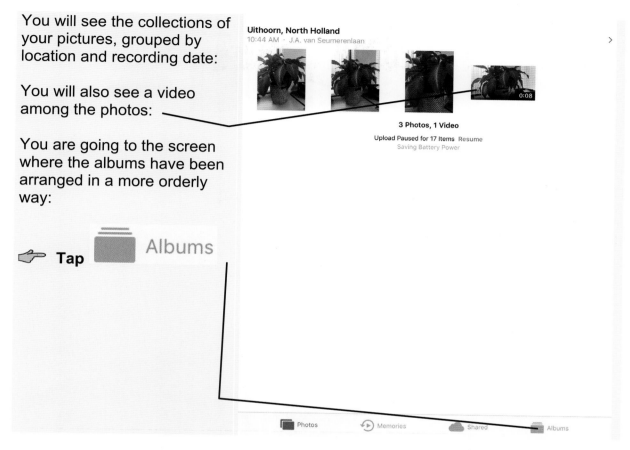

In the *Albums* view, the photos are sorted. You can compare an album to a folder that contains photos. The *Photos* app has a number of default albums. The app automatically recognizes the photos with people in it and places these in the *People* album. The location where the picture is taken is recognized as well, and these photos are placed in the *Places* album, arranged per location. There also is one album that contains all the photos. This is the album you are currently using:

👉 **Tap** Camera Roll

You may see **All Photos** instead.

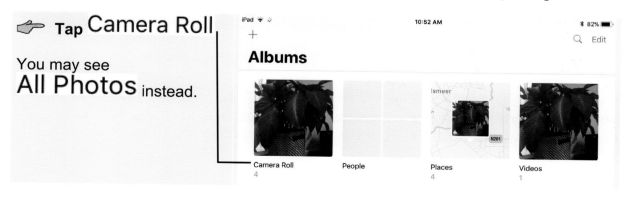

You will see the thumbnails of the pictures you have taken:

☞ **Tap the second photo**

The photo is displayed on a full screen. You may see a window with information:

☞ **If necessary, tap** Got It

This is how you browse to the next photo:

☞ **Swipe across the photo, from right to left**

You will see the next photo. You can go back to the previous photo:

☞ **Swipe across the photo, from left to right**

You can also zoom in on a photo:

 Move your thumb and index finger apart, on the screen

You will zoom in on the photo:

Note: the picture might become a bit blurry when you zoom in.

 Tip

Moving the photo
You can move the photo you have just zoomed in on, by dragging your finger across the screen.

This is how you zoom out again:

 Move your thumb and index finger towards each other, on the screen

You will again see the regular view of the photo. Look at some more views in the *Photos* app:

👉 **Tap the photo**

👉 **Tap** ❮ Camera Roll

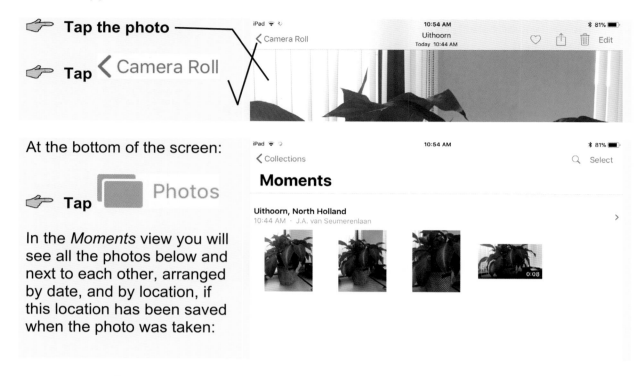

At the bottom of the screen:

👉 **Tap** ▢ Photos

In the *Moments* view you will see all the photos below and next to each other, arranged by date, and by location, if this location has been saved when the photo was taken:

By tapping ❮ Collections at the top, the view will become more compressed. If you have lots of photos, this view will make it easier to get an overview and find a specific photo.

👉 **Tap** ❮ Collections

You can compress the view even more by tapping ❮ Years.

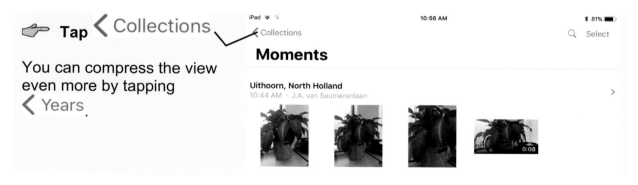

Go back to the previous view:

☞ **Tap the miniature**

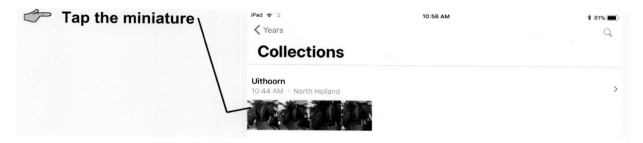

To show all the photos in larger size next to each other:

☞ **To the right of the**

photos, tap >

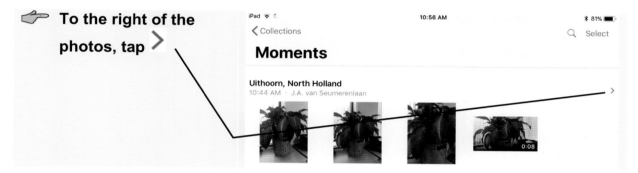

The photos are displayed in such a way that they look like a collage and the location is shown:

By dragging upwards across the screen, related photos are found, and you can add

photos to the 〔▶〕 Memories view. You open this view with the button at the bottom of the screen.

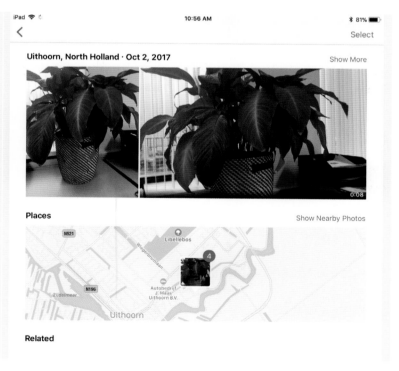

Go back to the Albums view:

☞ **Tap**  Albums

Tip
Delete a photo
You can easily delete a photo you have taken with the iPad from your iPad:

☞ **If necessary, tap the photo**

☞ **In the top right of your screen, tap** 🗑

☞ **Tap** Delete Photo

These photos will be stored in the album *Recently Deleted*. The photos or videos will be erased 30 days after being marked for deletion. Each item shows the days remaining. You can restore an item like this:

☞ **Open the folder** Recently Deleted

☞ **In the top right of your screen, tap** Select

If you would like to recover all items:

☞ **Tap** Recover All

To recover one or multiple items:

☞ **Tap one item or more photos or videos**

☞ **Tap** Recover Photo

6.4 Play a Video Recording

In *section 6.2 Shooting Videos* you have shot a short video with your iPad. You can view this video with the *Photos* app as well:

☞ **Tap** ‹ Albums

Select the Videos album:

☞ **Tap** Videos

☞ **Tap the video**

☞ **If necessary, turn your iPad a quarter turn, so it is in the horizontal position**

You will see your video. To play the video:

☞ **Tap**

The video will fill the screen:

☞ **Tap the screen**

You can see a pause button:

With this slider ▐, you can fast forward or rewind the video:

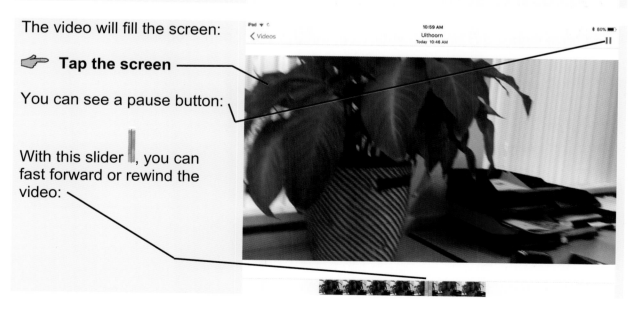

After playback, Edit is displayed, so you can still crop the video if you wish. You

will also see 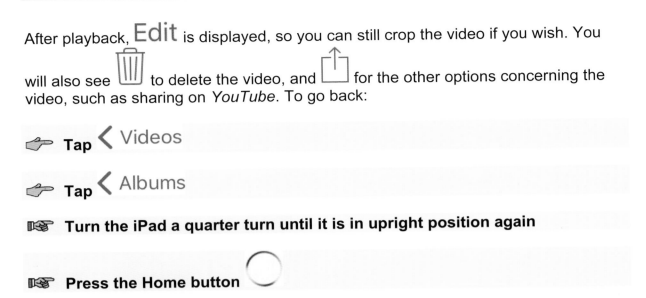 to delete the video, and for the other options concerning the video, such as sharing on *YouTube*. To go back:

Tap ❮ Videos

Tap ❮ Albums

☞ **Turn the iPad a quarter turn until it is in upright position again**

☞ **Press the Home button**

6.5 Copying Photos and Videos to the Computer

You can use *File Explorer* to copy the photos and video you have made with your iPad to your computer. You do this by inserting the supplied cable in your iPad and your computer's USB port:

☞ **Connect the iPad to the computer**

If you have installed *iTunes* on your computer, this program is opened:

☞ **If necessary, close *iTunes* ⬚¹⁶**

You can open *File Explorer* from the desktop:

Click

Your iPad will be detected by *Windows*, as if it were a digital camera:

☞ **Click** 🖳 This PC

☞ **Double-click your iPad's name**

Naturally, your own iPad will have a different name than shown here.

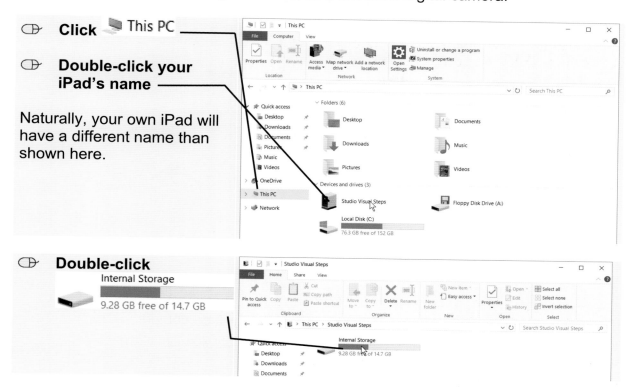

☞ **Double-click**

Internal Storage

9.28 GB free of 14.7 GB

The photos and video are stored in a folder called *DCIM*:

☞ **Double-click**

DCIM

☞ **Double-click**

100APPLE

You may see more or other subfolders in the *DCIM* folder. Possibly the photos are saved in a different folder on your own device.

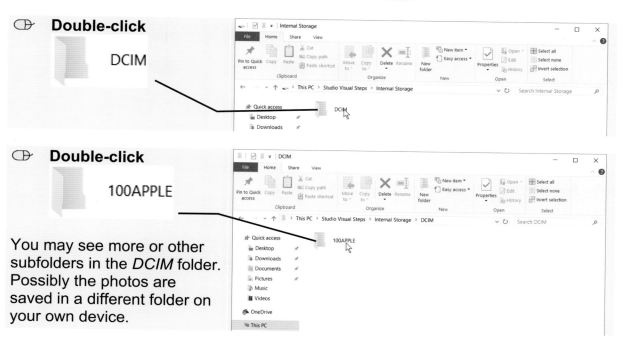

You will see the thumbnails of all the photos and videos on your iPad. You can copy these files to your computer, for example, to your *Pictures* folder:

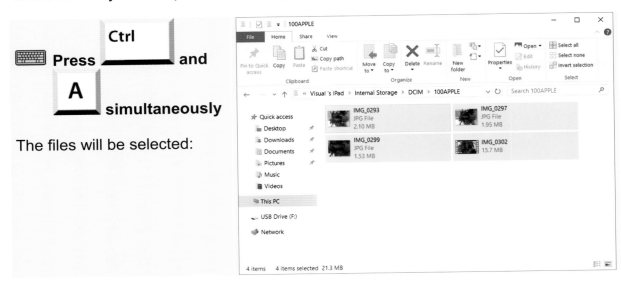

Press Ctrl and A simultaneously

The files will be selected:

If you drag the files to a folder on your computer, they will be copied:

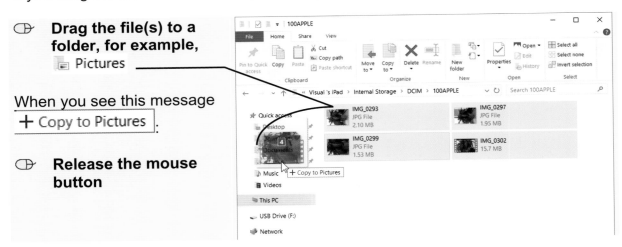

⊕ **Drag the file(s) to a folder, for example,** 📷 **Pictures**

When you see this message ┣ Copy to Pictures .

⊕ **Release the mouse button**

Now the files have been copied to your computer.

 Please note:
This method will only work if you copy photos from your iPad to your computer. You cannot transfer photos from your computer to your iPad in this way. In the next section you can read how to do this with *iTunes*.

☞ **Close *File Explorer*** ✂16

6.6 Copying Photos and Videos to Your iPad Through iTunes

Your iPad is a useful tool for showing your favorite pictures and videos to others. Actually, you can also use the photos and videos on your computer. This is done by synchronizing the folder containing the photos and videos with your iPad, through *iTunes*.

 Please note:

In this section we assume that *iTunes* is already installed on your computer, and that your iPad has already been connected to *iTunes* before. If this is not the case, you can read how to do this in *Appendix B Installing iTunes and Connecting the iPad to the Computer*.

The iPad is still connected to the computer. Open *iTunes*:

☞ **Open *iTunes* on your computer** 🦶**17**

☞ **Click** ▢

The *Summary* page is opened. To go to the *Photos* page:

☞ **Click** 📷 **Photos**

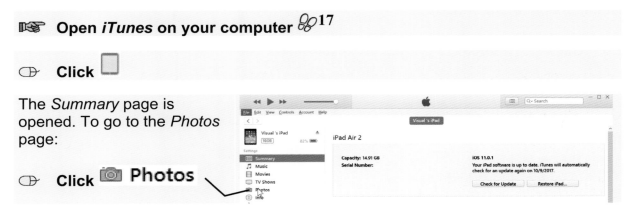

In this example, the photos from the *Pictures* folder will be synchronized. You will select a folder with your own pictures:

☞ **Check the box ☑ by** Sync Photos

The Pictures ↕ folder has already been selected:

In this example we will not synchronize all the subfolders of the *(My) Pictures* folder:

☞ **Check the radio button** ⦿ **next to** Selected folders

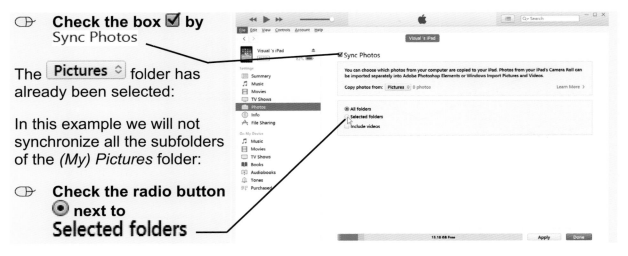

Tip

Videos
If you also want to synchronize the videos stored in this folder:

☞ **Check the box ☑ by Include videos**

Select the folder(s) you want to synchronize with your iPad. You will see different folders from the ones in this example, of course:

☞ **Check the box ☑ by the desired folder(s), for example Farm pictures**

At the bottom of the window:

☞ **Click** [**Apply**]

The synchronization has started:

You will see the progress of the synchronization:

Syncing Photos to "Visual 's iPad" (Step 4 of 4)
Copying photo 1 of 3

When you see the *Apple* logo the synchronization operation has finished:

After you have finished, you disconnect the iPad from the computer. If your iPad is still connected to your computer through *iTunes*, you can do it this way:

☞ **By Visual 's iPad , click** ⏏

If you no longer see your iPad in *iTunes*:

☞ **Disconnect your iPad from your computer**

☞ **Close *iTunes* 🔖16**

The photos are transferred to your iPad.

☞ **Open the *Photos* app** ✐**18**

At the bottom of the screen

☞ **If necessary, tap**

📁 Albums

The pile with the synchronized photos has been given the same name as the folder on your computer:

☞ **Tap the album** ────

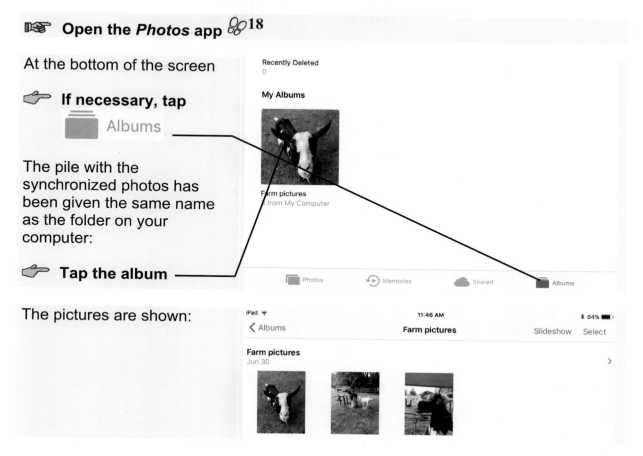

The pictures are shown:

You are going back to all the albums. In the top left-hand corner of the screen:

☞ **Tap** < Albums

6.7 Automatically Enhance a Photo

Sometimes, a photo can be too dark or too light. The auto-enhance function will let you make a 'ruined' photo look better in just a short while. This function adjusts the exposure and saturation of the photo. Just try it:

☞ **Open a photo** ✐**19**

The photo in this example
looks bleak and blurred:

 **If necessary, tap the
        photo**

 Tap Edit

To automatically enhance the
photo:

 Tap

Now the photo looks much
clearer and much livelier:

If you tap once again,
you will see the original photo
again.

You can also select a filter, in order to give a different atmosphere to the photo, with 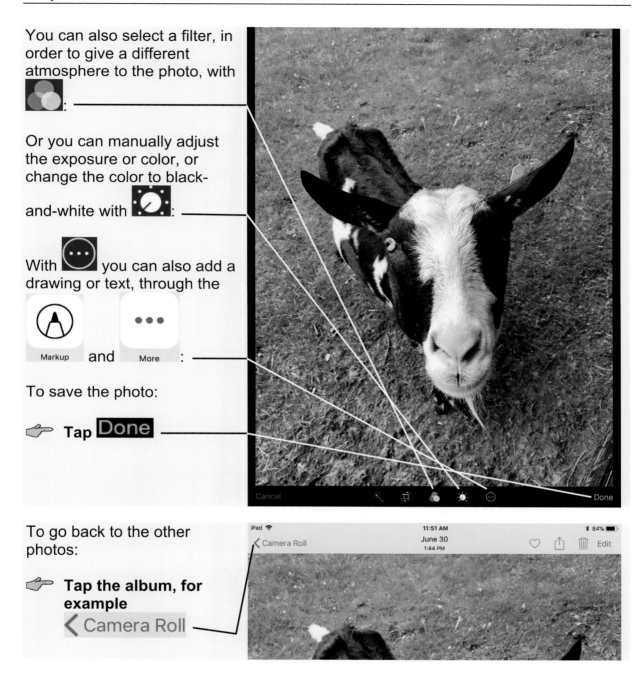 :

Or you can manually adjust the exposure or color, or change the color to black-and-white with :

With you can also add a drawing or text, through the

Markup and More :

To save the photo:

☞ **Tap** Done

To go back to the other photos:

☞ **Tap the album, for example**
❮ Camera Roll

The photo is saved.

Please note:

If you have transferred photos from your computer to your iPad you need to tap Duplicate and Edit before you can save the photo. Then a copy of the photo will be saved on the iPad.

If you want to view the picture you have saved, you do this:

☞ **Tap the name of the album at the top, for example,** ‹ Barcelona

☞ **Tap** ‹ Albums

☞ **Tap** ‹ Camera Roll

You will see the edited photo.

6.8 Crop a Photo

By cropping photos you can bring forward the most important part of the photo, or get rid of less pretty parts of the photo. You are going to crop a photo:

☞ **Open a photo** ✂[19]

☞ **If necessary, tap the photo**

☞ **Tap** Edit

At the bottom of the screen:

☞ **Tap**

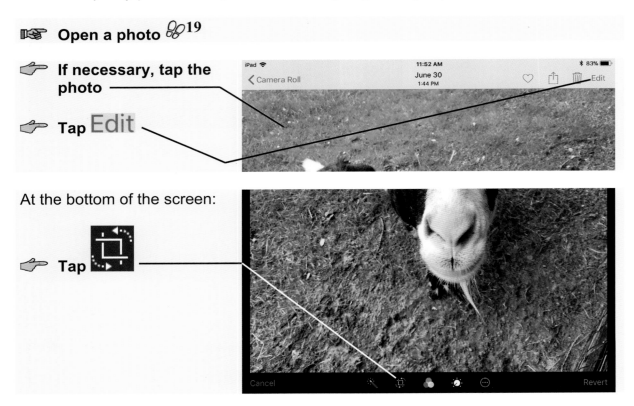

You will see a clear frame with nine boxes, all across the photo:

You can move this frame:

 Drag the bottom right-hand corner to the top left-hand corner a bit

You will see that the view of the photo is immediately adjusted to the frame.

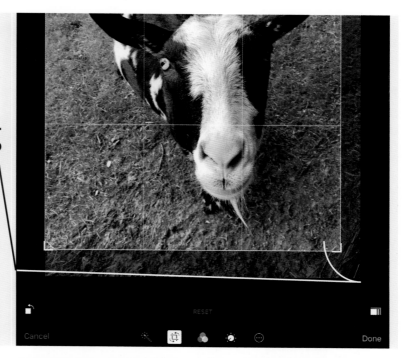

Now the aspect ratio of the photo is no longer correct. Select the desired ratio:

 Tap

The iPad's screen has a 3x4 ratio, if your photo is in landscape mode, this is 4:3:

 Tap 3:4

If desired, you can still straighten the photo by swiping your finger over

 or

turn with :

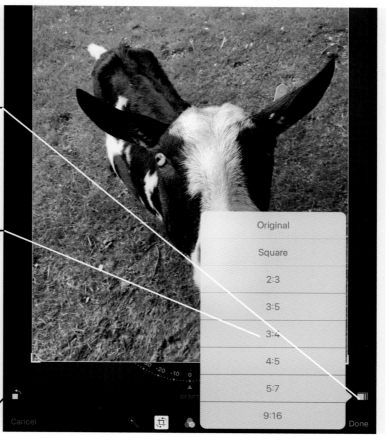

Original

Square

2:3

3:5

3:4

4:5

5:7

9:16

The cropped photo has been adjusted to the selected image ratio.

If necessary you can still move the photo, so the desired object is placed in the frame on the right spot.

With the RESET button you can restore the photo: ─

You may need to practice a bit in order to crop the photo as it should be.

To save the photo:

☞ Tap Done

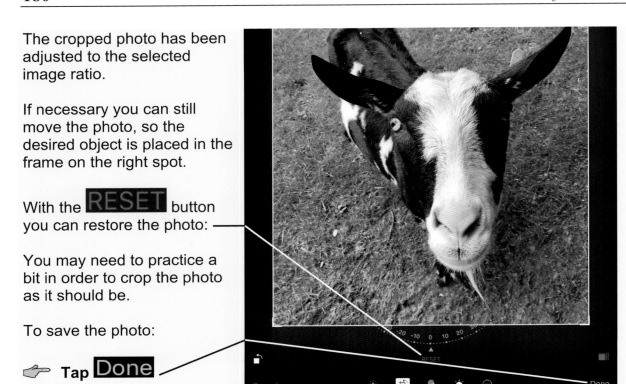

6.9 More Photo Options

There are more options available for photos:

☞ **If necessary, tap the photo** ─

Mark the photo as a favorite. The photo will be provided with a heart icon in the overview: ─

To view the other options:

☞ **Tap**

You can select multiple
photos at once, if you wish:

Share through *AirDrop*:

Share through other apps:

Show other apps, such as
play a slideshow, add to an
album, and use as wallpaper:

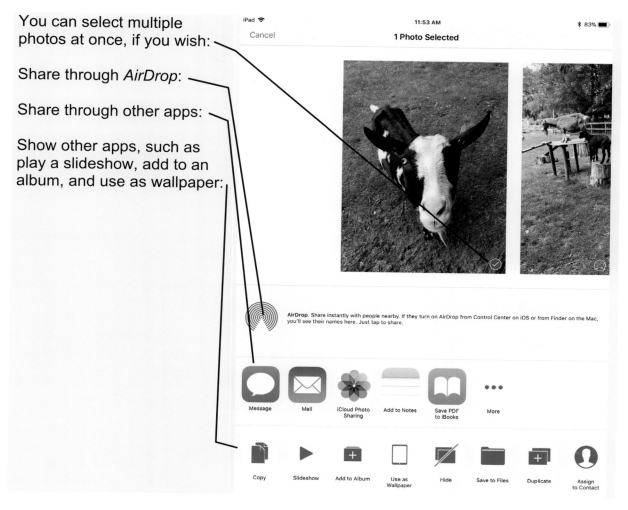

Now you are going back to all the photos. In the top left-hand corner of the screen:

☞ **Tap** ‹ Camera Roll

🖝 **Press the Home button** ◯

In this chapter you have learned more about the *Camera* and *Photos* app.

6.10 Background Information

Dictionary

AirDrop	A function that lets you quickly and easily share photos and other files with others next to you using Wi-Fi or Bluetooth.
AirPrint	An iPad function that allows you to print through a wireless connection, on a printer that supports *AirPrint*.
Camera	An app for taking pictures and shooting videos. With this app you can use both the front and back cameras on the iPad.
Camera Connection Kit	A set of two connectors, with which you can quickly and easily transfer photos from your digital camera to your iPad.
Digital zoom	A digital zoom function that enlarges a small part of the original picture. You will not see any additional details; all it does is make the pixels bigger. That is why the photo quality will diminish.
Photo Booth	An app that lets you take pictures with funny effects, such as an X-ray or kaleidoscope photo.
Photos	An app the lets you view the photos on the iPad.
Slideshow	Automatic display of a collection of pictures.

Source: iPad User Guide, Wikipedia.

6.11 Tips

 Tip

Self-portrait

You can also use the camera at the front of the iPad. For instance, for taking a picture of yourself. This is how you switch to the front camera:

 Tap

Now you will see the image recorded by the front camera. You can take a picture in the same way as you previously did with the back camera. Only, the front camera does not have a digital zoom option.

This is how you switch to the back camera again:

 Tap

 Tip

Make a screen shot

It is very easy to make a screen shot of your iPad. In this way you can save an image of a high score in a game, a nice message, or an error message, for example:

 Simultaneously press the Home button **and the Sleep/Wake button**

You will hear the clicking sound of a camera, and the screen shot is made. You can view this screen shot with the *Photos* app.

 Tip

Directly transfer photos to your iPad with the Camera Connection Kit

A very useful accessory to your iPad is the *Camera Connection Kit*. This is a set of two connectors that lets you quickly and easily transfer photos from your digital camera to your iPad. You can buy this Camera Connection Kit for about $29 (as of September 2017) at your Apple store.

Tip

Printing a photo
If you use a printer that supports the *AirPrint* function, you can print the photos on your iPad through a wireless connection. In this example you are printing a photo, but in a similar way, you can also print notes or web pages. This is how you print a photo on your iPad when a photo is already opened:

☞ **Tap** ⬆,   Print

Select the right printer:

☞ **Tap**
 Select Printer

☞ **Tap the printer you want to use**

Here you can change the number of copies to print:

You may see more options, depending on the type of printer you use:

☞ **Tap** 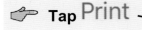 Print

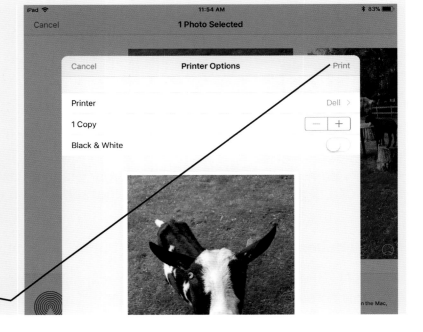

Tip

Photo Booth

The *Photo Booth* app allows you to add different types of effects to your photo right as you are taking the picture. You can use both cameras on the iPad with this app. This is how you open the *Photo Booth* app:

☞ **Tap** Photo Booth

You will see examples of the different effects:

☞ **Tap an effect, for example**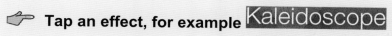

You will see a larger image of this effect. Now you can take a picture:

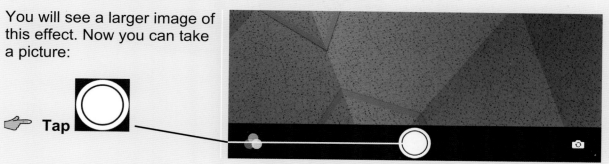

☞ **Tap**

With you can switch to the back camera. With ◖ you can display the opening screen of the *Photo Booth* app.

 Tip

Organize your photos in albums

You can create albums for your photos directly on your iPad. When you add a photo to a new album, you are actually adding a link to the photo from the Camera Roll album to the new one. By sorting your photos into albums, it makes it easier to find a series of photos about a specific subject later on. You can create a new album like this:

☞ **Tap**

- Continue on the next page -

You will see the albums on your iPad:

To create a new album:

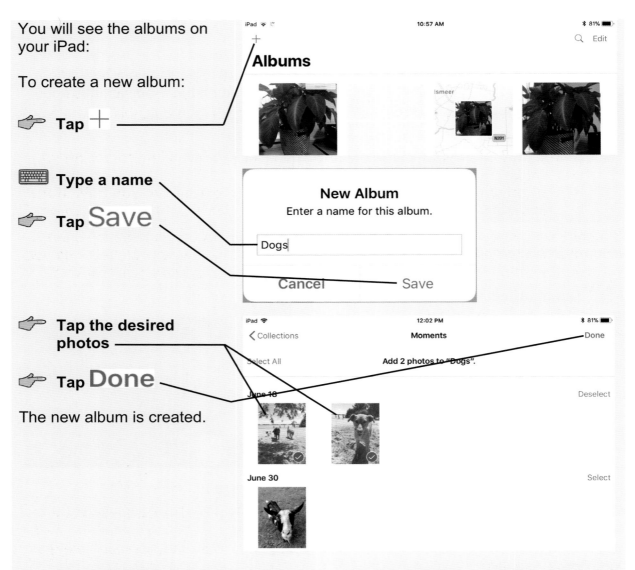

👉 **Tap** +

⌨ **Type a name**

👉 **Tap** Save

New Album

Enter a name for this album.

Dogs

Cancel   Save

👉 **Tap the desired photos**

👉 **Tap** Done

The new album is created.

If you want to delete an album on your iPad, you need to do this as follows. You will only delete the album; the photos will still be stored on your iPad.
Please note: you can only delete the albums you created on your iPad yourself.

👉 **Tap** Edit
👉 **By the album, tap**
👉 **Tap** Delete
👉 **Tap** Done

Tip

Delete synchronized photos and videos

If you have second thoughts and you do not want to save one or multiple synchronized photos on your iPad, you will need to delete these through *iTunes*. You can do this in several ways. If you want to delete just a few pictures, this is what you need to do:

☞ **Delete or move the unwanted photo from the synchronized folder on your computer**

☞ **Synchronize the folder with your iPad once more, just like you have done in *section 6.6 Copying Photos and Videos to Your iPad Through iTunes***

Synchronizing means that the content of the iPad folder will be made equal to the content of the folder on your computer. The photos that have been deleted or moved will also disappear from the iPad. You can also delete one or more synchronized folders:

⊕ **Uncheck the box ☑ by the folder you no longer wish to synchronize, for example,**
Farm pictures

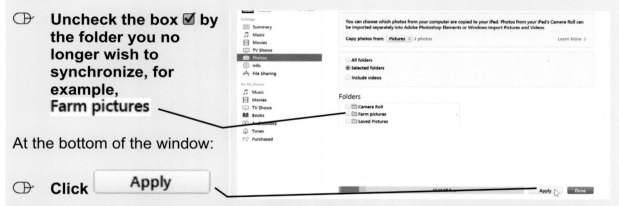

At the bottom of the window:

⊕ **Click** Apply

The synchronization operation has started and the folder is deleted from your iPad.

If you do not want to synchronize any photos at all with your iPad, you can delete all the photos, like this:

⊕ **Uncheck the box ☑ by**
Sync Photos

⊕ **Click** Remove Photos

⊕ **Click** Apply

The synchronization operation has started and all synchronized photos will be deleted.

Tip

Different video formats
The iPad only supports a limited number of video file formats: .M4V, .MP4, .MOV, .M-JPEG and .AVI. The video you want to play may have a different format.
An option is to download an app that is capable of playing all sorts of video file formats, such as the *Movie Player* or *Good Player* app. These apps can be purchased in the *App Store*.

7. Changing Settings

In the previous chapters you have become acquainted with the various options and apps on the iPad. Many of these apps and functions can be adjusted according to your preferences. In this chapter you will learn more about some of these settings.

For example, you will read about setting up *iCloud*, the online storage service offered by Apple. Here you can save files and data in order to view them on other devices, such as an iPhone. And if you have set up *iCloud*, this will also serve as a backup, in case something goes wrong with your iPad, or if it is stolen.

When you set up your iPad you may also have set a passcode. But you can also let the iPad scan your fingerprint and use Touch ID to unlock your device. Besides, you can set the time period after which the iPad is locked, in case you do not use it for a while.

Apart from this there are some settings that protect your privacy. You will see which apps have access to your location or to other data, such as your contacts. And you can also determine what is displayed in the *Notification Center* and in the widgets.

Furthermore, you will view the settings for the background. Of course, there are lots of other settings you can change. With the knowledge you have gained in this chapter you will be able to view and use these settings later on.

In this chapter you will learn how to:

- set up *iCloud*;
- change and disable the passcode;
- set the Touch ID;
- set the automatic lock;
- activate location services and access to your data;
- set up the *Notification Center*;
- set widgets;
- set the background.

☞ **Press the Home button**

If you have another *iOS* device, such as an iPhone or another iPad:

☞ **Follow the steps in this section once more to set up your other device**

You have seen that various components can be enabled or disabled while setting up *iCloud*. When you enable a component, some of the data of the corresponding app will be saved in *iCloud* and automatically synchronized between all the devices on which you use *iCloud*.

These are the data that are saved for each app:

☁ iCloud Drive	*iCloud Drive* is the online USB stick in *iCloud*. In *iCloud Drive* you can save all kinds of files, also if these files are not created for the Apple software. These files are synchronized with all the devices on which you have enabled your *iCloud Drive*. On all the other devices you can view the files and manage them through the *iCloud* website www.icloud.com. On the iPad you can use the special *Files* app to view the files that are stored on *iCloud Drive*.
✿ Photos	In the *iCloud* photo library, all the photos and videos are stored from all the devices on which the *iCloud* photo library has been enabled. The photos and videos are synchronized between all the devices. You can view the *iCloud* photo library on the Mac and *Windows* computer, and manage it through the *iCloud* website www.icloud.com.
✉ Mail	This feature in *iCloud* can only be used with the special free @icloud.com or @me.com email account. Read, sent, and deleted messages are saved in *iCloud* and automatically synchronized between all your devices.
Contacts	Contact data that you enter or modify.
Calendars	Appointments that you enter or modify.
Reminders	Reminders that you enter or modify.
Safari	• The bookmarks (favorites) that you enter or modify. • The tabs that are opened in *Safari* on your other devices.

🏠	**Home**	The settings you enter in the *Home* app, in order to control various accessories in your home, are saved in your *iCloud* account. You can also share the settings with others, through your *iCloud* account.
	Game Center	*Game Center* is a service provided by Apple that lets you exchange data from *iOS* games. Sign in with your *iCloud* account, and your data will be saved there.
	Siri	*Siri* is linked to *iCloud*, which makes it possible to synchronize your preferences with other devices.
	Notes	The notes you make in the *Notes* app are saved in *iCloud* and automatically synchronized between your devices.
🔄	**iCloud Backup**	Every day *iCloud* will automatically create backup copies through Wi-Fi, of all your devices (iPad, iPhone and iPod touch) whenever you turn these on, lock them, or connect them to a power source. If you have saved a backup copy of the information on the device in *iCloud*, you can very easily set up a new device, or restore the data on one of your existing devices.
🔑	**Keychain**	The Keychain is a useful service that lets you save your passwords and credit card data online. These data will be encrypted and this way you will have all the passwords available on all the devices that use the same *iCloud* account. They can be filled in automatically when you need them.
	Find My iPad	Option on your iPad, iPhone, and Mac to locate your device on a map. By signing in with the *iCloud* website with an Internet browser, for example, *Safari* or *Edge*, you can display your iPad, iPhone, or Mac on a map. This option will let you remotely lock your device or erase the data, and you can display a message to the person who finds your device.
☁️	**Set Up Family Sharing...**	With *Family Sharing* you can share purchases in the *iTunes Store*, *iBooks Store* and *App Store* with at most six members of your family without sharing your accounts. But only if all the purchases have been paid for with the same credit card. The purchases done by the kids can be directly approved through the device of the parents. You can also share photos, or a family calendar.

Share My Location   If you become a member of a *Family Sharing* group, you can automatically share your locations. For example, if you want to know if your child has already come home, you use the apps *Find My Friends* or *Messages* to keep an eye on things. You can temporarily stop sharing your location by using the switch for *Share My Location* in the *iCloud* settings.

☞ **Press the Home button**

The *Files* app works together with *iCloud*. If *iCloud* is set up on your iPad, you can view the files with this app:

At the bottom of the screen:

☞ **Tap**

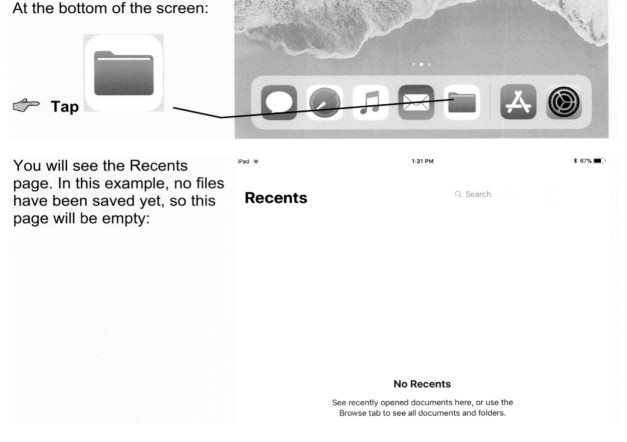

You will see the Recents page. In this example, no files have been saved yet, so this page will be empty:

iPad 🔋   1:31 PM   🔋 67% ■

Recents   🔍 Search

No Recents

See recently opened documents here, or use the
Browse tab to see all documents and folders.

You are going to open a web page, where you can download a file and save it:

☞ **Press the Home button**

☞ **Open the *Safari* app** ⌇⌇²⁰

☞ **Open the web page www.visualsteps.com/ onenote2016** ⌇⌇²¹

To open the PDF file:

☞ **Tap** 📄 Table of contents

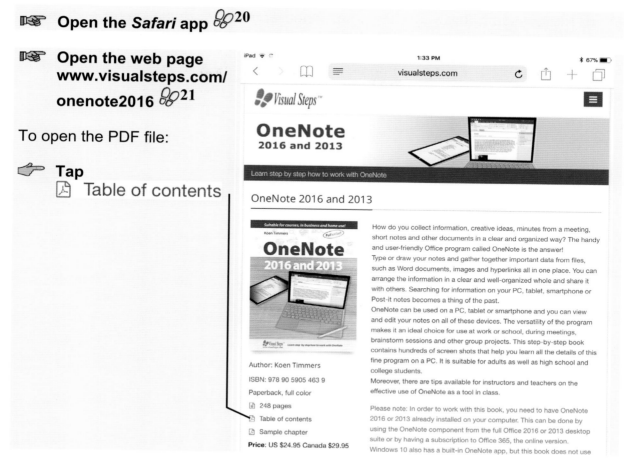

To save the file:

☞ **Tap** ⬆️

☞ **Drag across the bottom options, from right to left**

☞ **Tap** Save to Files

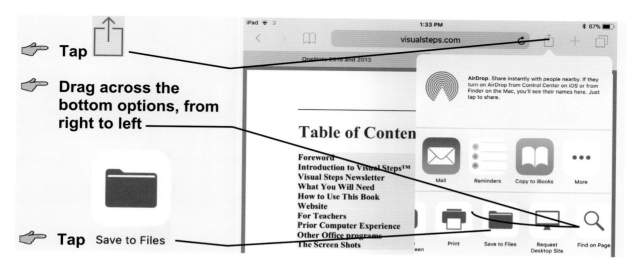

Select the location where you want to save the file. In this example we have chosen *iCloud Drive*. When we were writing this book, it was not possible to choose On My iPad.

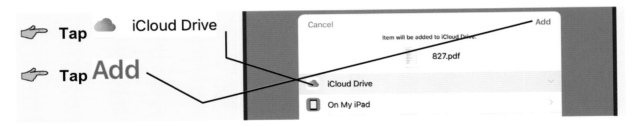

☞ **Tap** ☁ **iCloud Drive**

☞ **Tap Add**

Go back to the home screen:

☞ **Press the Home button**

☞ **Open the *Files* app** 👣²²

You will see the file at the Recents page:

View the Browse page. At the bottom of the screen:

☞ **Tap** 📁 **Browse**

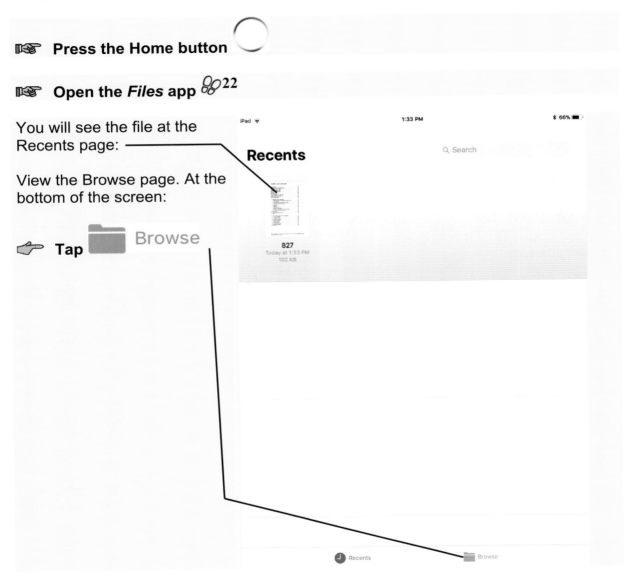

Here the files are displayed from various preset locations. In this example, *iCloud* is the only location that has been set: ───

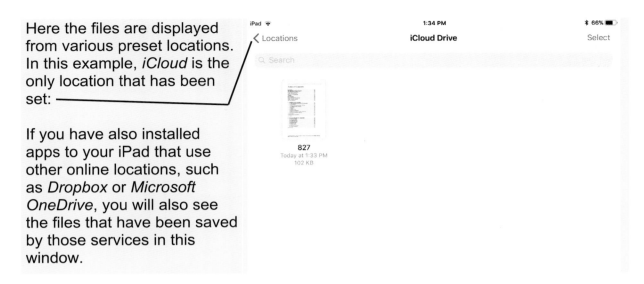

If you have also installed apps to your iPad that use other online locations, such as *Dropbox* or *Microsoft OneDrive*, you will also see the files that have been saved by those services in this window.

Go back to the home screen again:

☞ **Press the Home button**

7.2 Modify and Turn Off a Passcode

You can modify the six-digit passcode and change it into an alphanumeric code, or a numeric code. This is how you do it:

☞ **If necessary, open the *Settings* app** ✂ **1**

☞ **Tap**
   Touch ID & Passcode

⌨ **Type your passcode**

☞ **Tap**
   Change Passcode

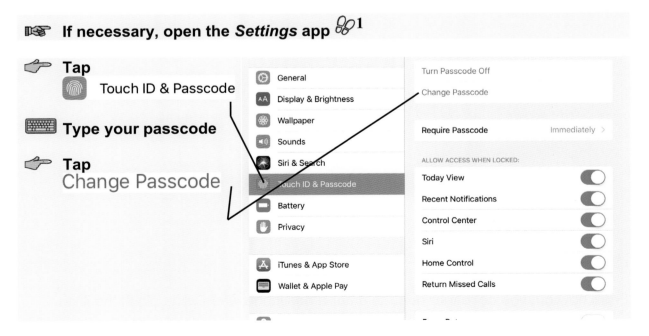

⌨ **Type your passcode**

👉 **Tap**
   Passcode Options

👉 **Tap**
   6-Digit Numeric Code

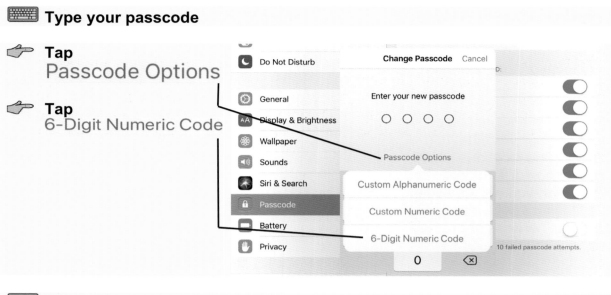

⌨ **Type a six-digit passcode**

⌨ **Retype the passcode**

The code has changed. If it bothers you to have to enter the passcode when you unlock your iPad, you can turn off this option. But keep in mind that others will be able to use your iPad too, if you do this:

👉 **Tap**
   Turn Passcode Off

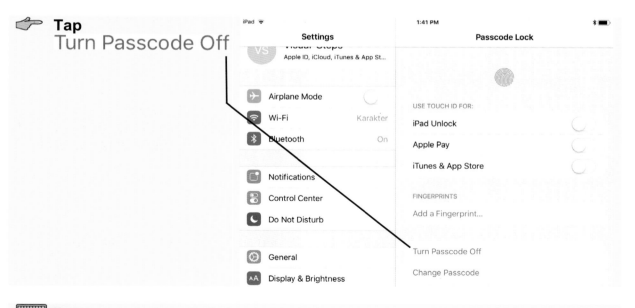

⌨ **Retype your passcode**

From now on, you no longer need to enter a passcode when you unlock the iPad.

7.3 Setting Up Touch ID

Most new models of iPads are equipped with Touch ID. On the device, the Home button contains a fingerprint scanner that allows you to do different things. First, you can quickly unlock your device with your finger without the required passcode. Also, you can quickly log on to apps that are suitable for that purpose. Touch ID can be set during the installation of a new iPad. But it can also be set up later in the *Settings* app.

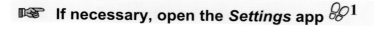 **If necessary, open the *Settings* app** $\mathscr{OO}$¹

☞ **Tap** 🔲 Touch ID & Passcode

If you only see the 🔒 Passcode option in *Settings*, this means the Touch ID feature is not available on your device. Only the newer models of the iPad are equipped with a fingerprint scanner and Touch ID.

⌨ **Type your passcode**

☞ **Tap** Add a Fingerprint...

Now you see some information on adding a fingerprint. You can proceed:

 **Place your finger, for example your thumb, on** ◯

iOS scans your finger. The idea is that you lift your finger briefly and rotate a little when the device vibrates. The red lines in the signed fingerprint indicate how much of your fingerprint is scanned already. Unfortunately, we cannot show any pictures of this process.

☞ **Tap** Continue

iOS will proceed with the scanning. Again, you have to lift and rotate your finger briefly when the device vibrates.

☞ **Tap** Continue

The fingerprint is now added, and is called 'Finger 1'. The fingerprint is now ready to use. In the future, you can unlock your iPad after you press the Home button.

If you wish you can add more fingers, for example, of your other hand, by tapping Add a Fingerprint... .

7.4 Set Auto-Lock

By default, the iPad will lock and go into sleep mode after two minutes, if you do not use it, or it is left unattended. This setting will save energy, but maybe you would prefer to keep the iPad on for a little longer:

☞ **If necessary, open the *Settings* app** 👣**1**

☞ **Tap** AA Display & Brightness

☞ **Tap** Auto-Lock

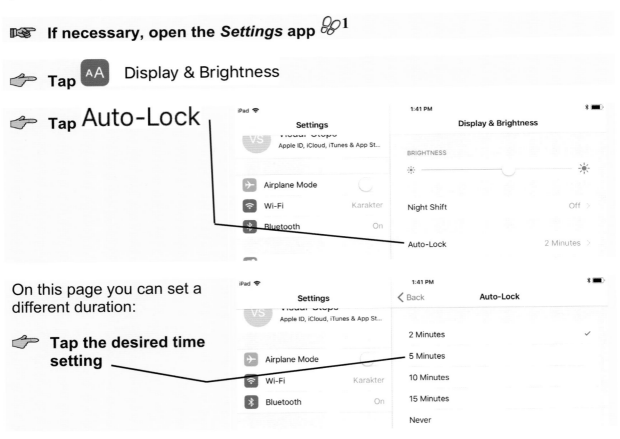

On this page you can set a different duration:

☞ **Tap the desired time setting**

7.5 Location Services and Access to Your Data

In the *Settings* app you can modify or turn off the location services for various apps:

☞ **If necessary, open the *Settings* app** ✌¹

On the left-hand side of the screen:

☞ **Tap** ✋ Privacy

☞ **Tap** 🧭 Location Services

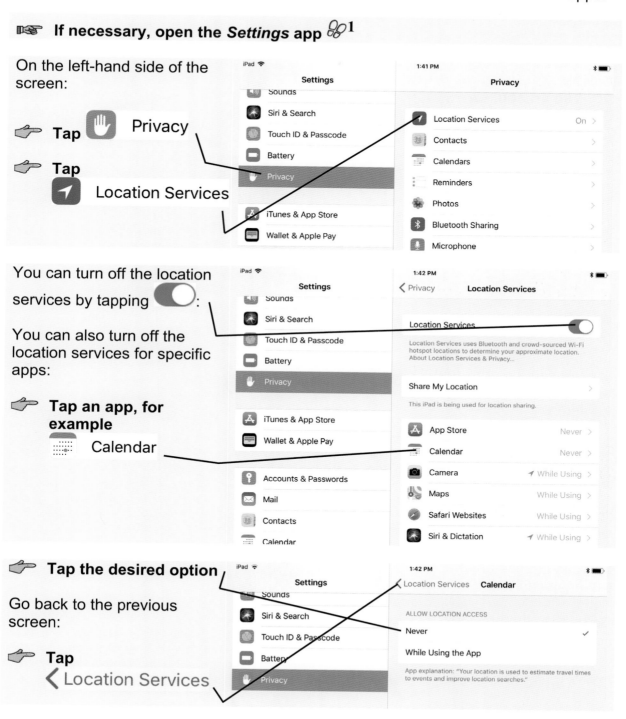

You can turn off the location services by tapping ⬤:

You can also turn off the location services for specific apps:

☞ **Tap an app, for example** ▦ Calendar

☞ **Tap the desired option**

Go back to the previous screen:

☞ **Tap** ‹ Location Services

It is may also occur that apps can access certain data on your iPad, depending on whether you have given permission for this at an earlier stage. An app such as *Facebook*, for instance, may have asked for permission to access your contacts, so you can add new contacts to your *Facebook* account. This is how you view these settings:

☞ **Tap** ‹ Privacy

☞ **Tap an app, for example** Contacts

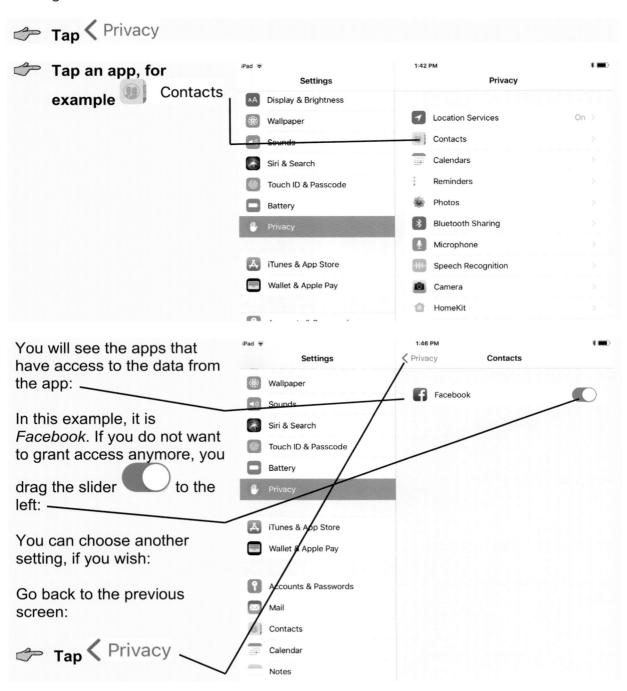

You will see the apps that have access to the data from the app:

In this example, it is *Facebook*. If you do not want to grant access anymore, you drag the slider to the left:

You can choose another setting, if you wish:

Go back to the previous screen:

☞ **Tap** ‹ Privacy

7.6 Setting Up the Notification Center

In *Chapter 1 The iPad* you have already gotten to know the *Notification Center*. In the *Settings* app you can select which notifications should be displayed per app in the *Notification Center*.

☞ **If necessary, open the *Settings* app** 🐾¹

👉 **Tap** 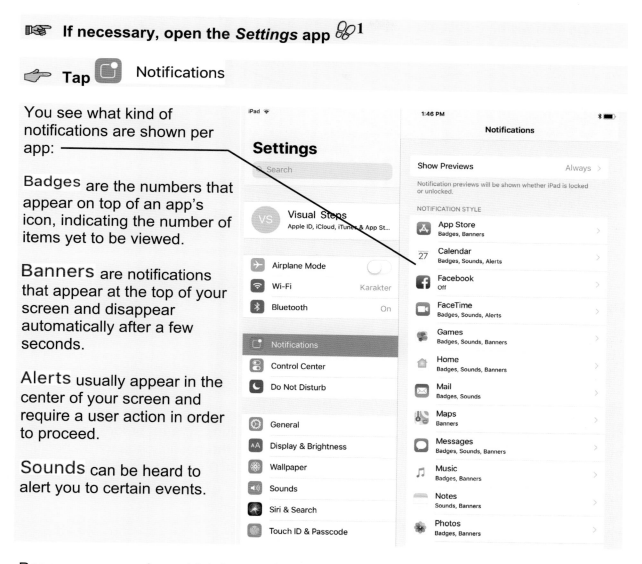 Notifications

You see what kind of notifications are shown per app: ———————

Badges are the numbers that appear on top of an app's icon, indicating the number of items yet to be viewed.

Banners are notifications that appear at the top of your screen and disappear automatically after a few seconds.

Alerts usually appear in the center of your screen and require a user action in order to proceed.

Sounds can be heard to alert you to certain events.

Per app you can view which types of notifications are set, and change this, if you wish:

👉 **Tap** Reminders
Badges, Sounds, Alerts**, for example**

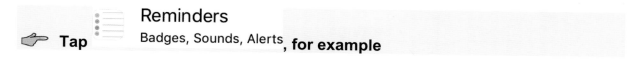

In this example, notifications are allowed:

If the volume is turned on, a sound is played:

A badge will be displayed on the app symbol on the home screen:

A message is displayed on the lock screen, in the history, and as a banner:

The banners can be displayed all the time or just temporarily:

You can also choose to always display the preview, or only if the device is unlocked:

☞ **Select the desired settings**

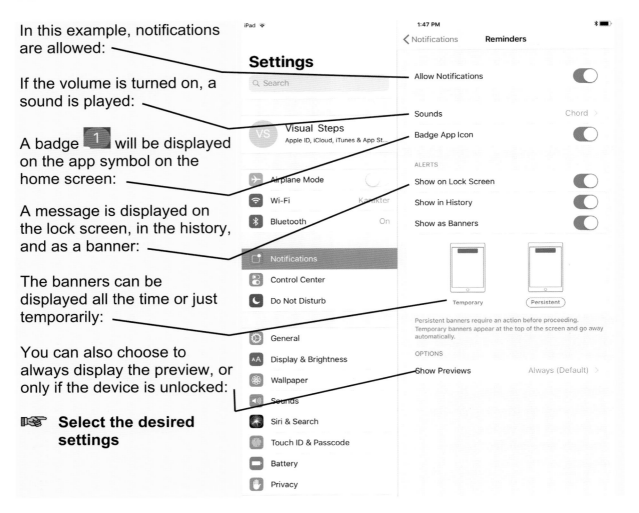

Please note:
The *Notification Center* can also be accessed from the lock screen, before you enter the access code. To prevent other people from viewing the notifications for a specific app, you can keep the option to Show on Lock Screen off.

Tip
Disable all the notifications
If you do not want so see any notifications for a certain app, you can disable this function like this:

☞ **By** Allow Notifications, **tap**

The slider turns to   .

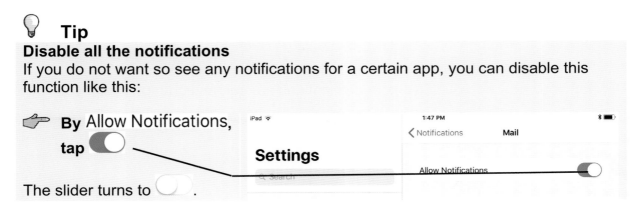

☞ **Press the Home button**

7.7 Setting Up Widgets

Widgets are tools for getting access to information quickly without the need of opening an app. The widgets are prominent in the *Notification Center*. You can use the standard widgets, but also add additional widgets.

☞ **Swipe from left to right over the screen**

☞ **Drag up from the bottom of the screen**

☞ **Tap**
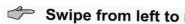

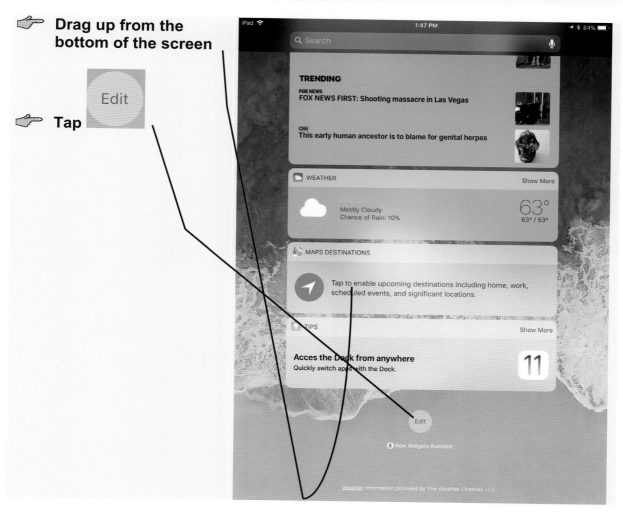

In the menu that appears, widgets that are shown will have a ⊖ button next to their name. To add a widget:

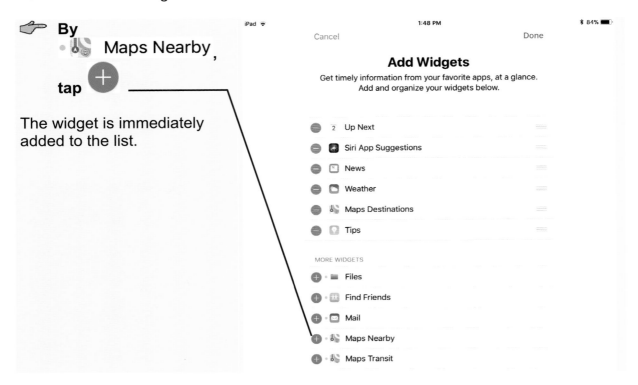

☞ **By**
   • 🗺️ **Maps Nearby**,

   tap ⊕

The widget is immediately added to the list.

It is also possible to rearrange or delete widgets. The widgets with a ⊖ to the left of the name can be moved up or down. They will be subsequently shown in a different order in the *Notification Center*:

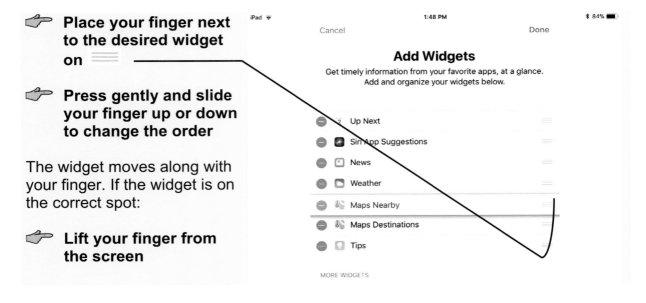

☞ **Place your finger next to the desired widget on** ≡

☞ **Press gently and slide your finger up or down to change the order**

The widget moves along with your finger. If the widget is on the correct spot:

☞ **Lift your finger from the screen**

It is also possible to remove a widget, so that it no longer appears in the *Notification Center*. This actually only deactivates the widget, they are not deleted from your iPad, but simply not displayed anymore:

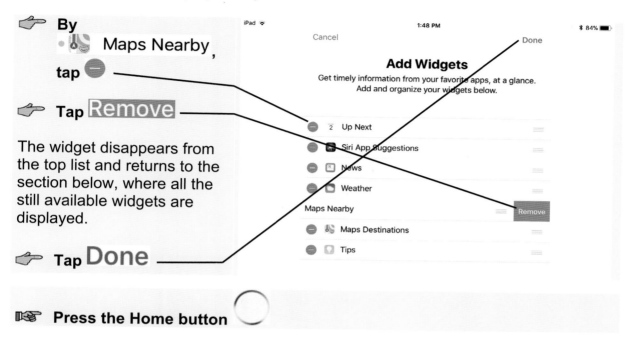

👉 **By** • 🌡 **Maps Nearby** , **tap** ⊖

👉 **Tap Remove**

The widget disappears from the top list and returns to the section below, where all the still available widgets are displayed.

👉 **Tap Done**

☞ **Press the Home button** ◯

7.8 Setting the Background

This is how you change the background image (wallpaper) on the home screen and the lock screen. You can use a standard image or one of your own photos:

☞ **If necessary, open the *Settings* app** ✂️[1]

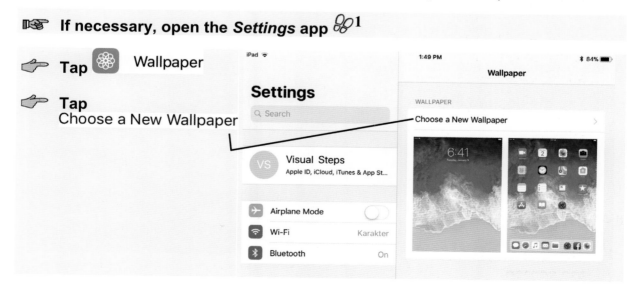

👉 **Tap** 🌐 **Wallpaper**

👉 **Tap Choose a New Wallpaper**

Dynamic images will move when you move the iPad. You select a still image:

Here you can select your own image, if you want to use this:

To view the stills:

☞ **Tap** Stills

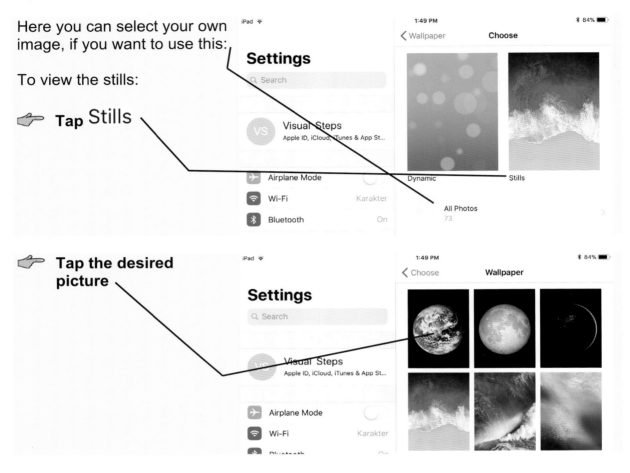

☞ **Tap the desired picture**

You can choose to display the image on the home screen, on the lock screen, or on both. And you can also turn the perspective zoom on or off.

At the bottom of the screen:

☞ **Tap the desired choice**

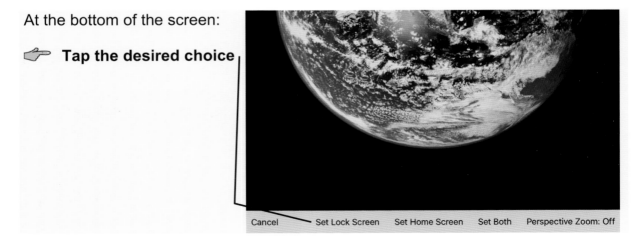

☞ **Press the Home button**

In this chapter you have looked at a couple of settings. If you look at the left-hand side of the *Settings* app, you will see many more categories for which you can change the settings:

For example, here you see the categories for the screen, sounds, *Siri*, and the battery:

👉 **Drag upwards across the left-hand side of the screen**

In these categories you will find settings for specific apps:

👉 **Tap** 🧭 **Safari, for example**

You will see the settings:

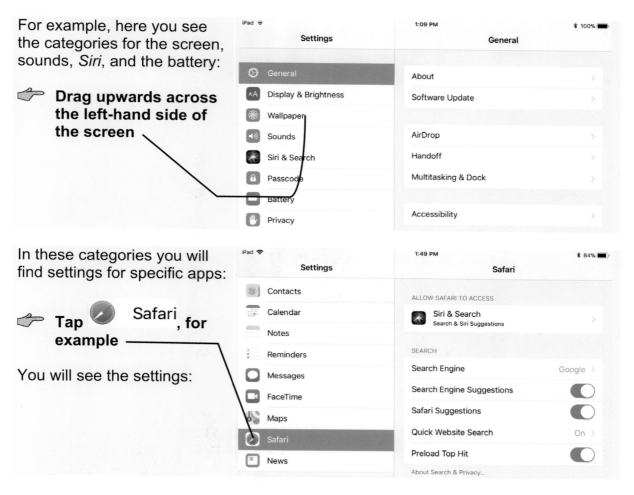

If you wish you can view or modify the settings per category or per app.

In this chapter you have learned how to set up *iCloud*, and read about the components you can link to this online storage service. You have also seen how to enable various settings that secure your iPad, among other things. Of course, there are many more settings you can change in the *Settings* app. If you wish, you can take a look in your own time, and if you like these settings.

7.9 Background Information

Dictionary

Auto-lock	A default function that makes sure the iPad is locked after two minutes of inactivity.
iCloud	The online storage service offered by Apple.
Files	App on the iPad where you can find your files.

Source: User Guide iPad, Wikipedia.

7.10 Tips

 Tip

Quickly display recent files

A useful option is the possibility of quickly displaying recent files that are stored in the *Files* app, without needing to open the app:

☞ **Press your finger to**

, just a bit longer than usual

You will see the files in a small window:

You open the file by tapping it.

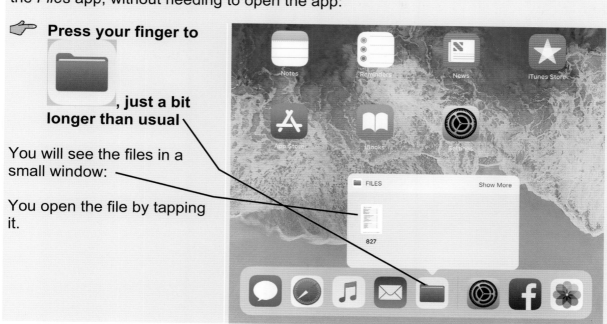

 Tip

Searching for settings

If you cannot find a specific setting, you can use the search box:

☞ **If necessary, drag downwards across the left-hand side of the screen**

⌨ **Type the keyword**

You will see the search results:

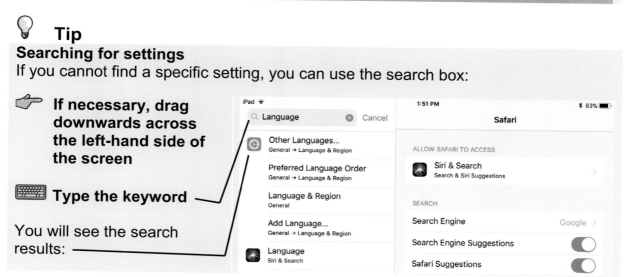

Notes

Write your notes down here.

8. The iPhone

Maybe you also have an iPhone apart from your iPad. Working on an iPhone is very similar to using an iPad, but some apps may look different on the iPhone, due to the different size of the screen. For example, the *Settings* app on the iPad has a screen that consists of two parts, while the same app takes up a single screen on the iPhone and you will skip from screen to screen on that device.

In apps such as *Safari* and *Calendar*, you will see certain buttons appear in another place on the screen, or you might need to use a certain button to reach another screen that will display the button you were looking for. But after you have practiced using the *iOS* operating system for a while and are used to it, you will be able to use the iPad and iPhone without any difficulty.

There are also some specific apps that you will mainly use on the iPhone, such as apps for making phone calls, and sending and reading text messages.

In this chapter you will learn:

- about the main differences between the iPad and iPhone;
- how to make phone calls with the iPhone;
- how to make a video call with *FaceTime*;
- how to use the *Messages* app;
- about the use of mobile data.

 Please note:

In order to execute all the steps in this chapter, you will need to have an iPhone. You can also execute *Section 8.2 Making Calls* if you have an iPad with 3G/4G, since the screen looks very similar. You can also execute *Section 8.3 Making Video Calls with FaceTime* on the iPad. And *Section 8.4 The Messages App* is suitable for the iPad as well, because you can use your *Apple ID*.

8.1 Main Differences Between the iPad and the iPhone

In this section you will see some examples of screens that are different on the iPhone. The home screen of the iPhone looks similar to the screen of the iPad. But the apps may differ. Let us take a look at the *Safari* app:

☞ **If necessary, wake up the iPhone from sleep mode or turn it on** $\mathscr{P}^2$

☞ **Tap**

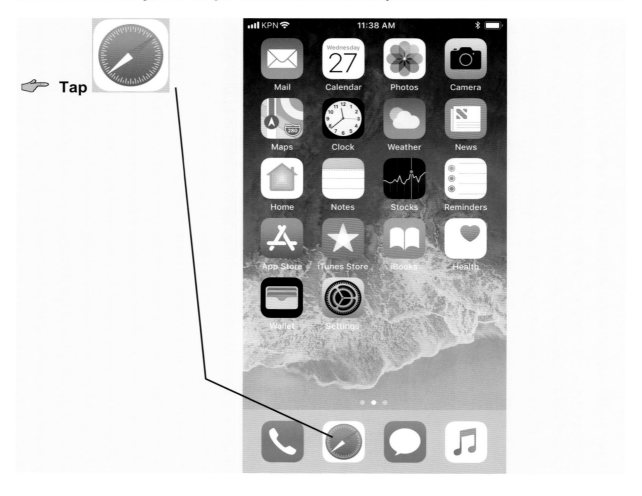

Due to the different ratio of the iPhone screen, not all the buttons will sit at the top of the screen. That is why you see these buttons at the bottom of the screen:

Nor will you see all the open tabs, in case you have opened multiple tabs:

👉 **Tap**

Now the tabs are displayed, and you will also see the button that opens a new tab:

Go back again:

👉 Tap **Done**

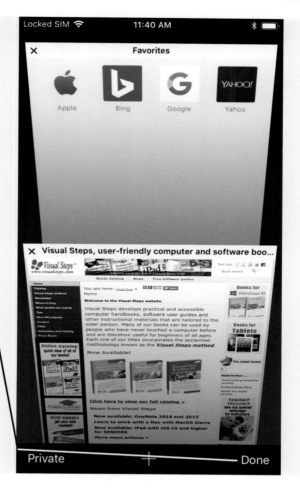

If you have bookmarked your favorite websites, these will be displayed on the left-hand side of your iPad. On the iPhone, a separate screen is used:

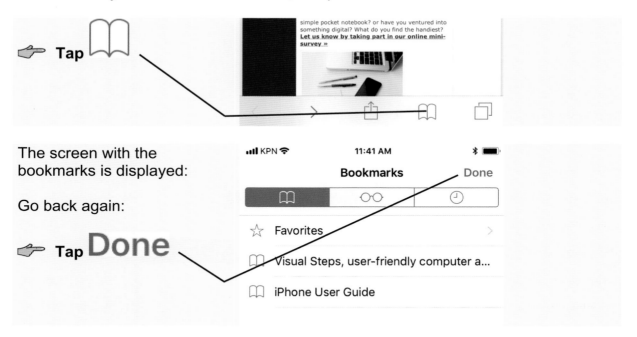

The screen with the bookmarks is displayed:

Go back again:

☞ Tap **Done**

You will encounter these kind of differences in the other apps too. You might need to search a while for the relevant button or function, but these are usually still available.

🖙 **Press the Home button**

The *Settings* app also consists of two parts on the iPad. On the left you see the categories, and on the right you see the settings you can change. On the iPhone you need to leaf from one screen to another:

☞ Tap Settings

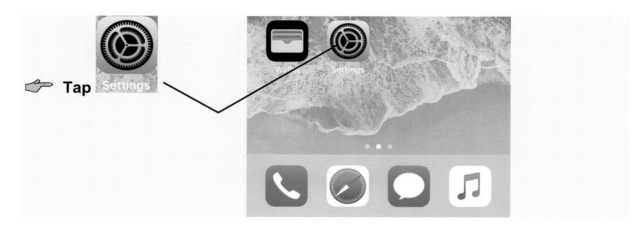

You will see the various categories, and also the apps for which you can change the settings, if you drag from bottom to top:

☞ **Swipe upwards across the screen**

☞ **Tap** Wallpaper

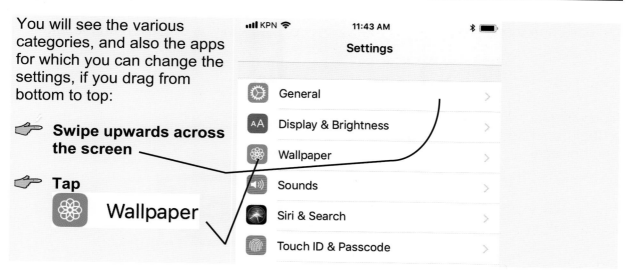

At once, the options are displayed on a new screen:

At the top you can see what the previous screen looked like:

Open the next screen:

☞ **Tap** Choose a New Wallpa

The screen with the wallpaper options is displayed:

Go back again:

☞ **Tap** ‹ Wallpaper

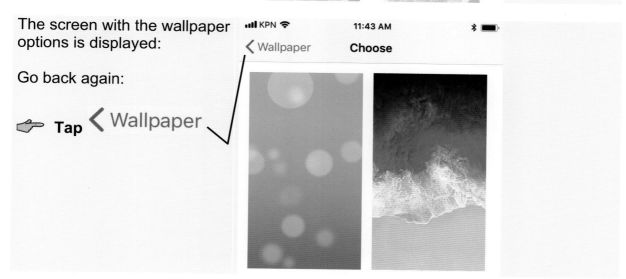

Go back one more screen:

Tap

You will notice that you need to leaf from one screen to another again.

Display all the opened apps:

Quickly press the Home button twice

A screen with the most recent apps is displayed. This screen looks different as well. Here you will only see recently opened apps. Drag from left to right in order to switch between opened apps. By dragging upwards, you close the apps. By pressing the Home button, you go back to the home screen:

You will see the recently opened apps:

Press the Home

button

The *Control Center* looks a bit different as well:

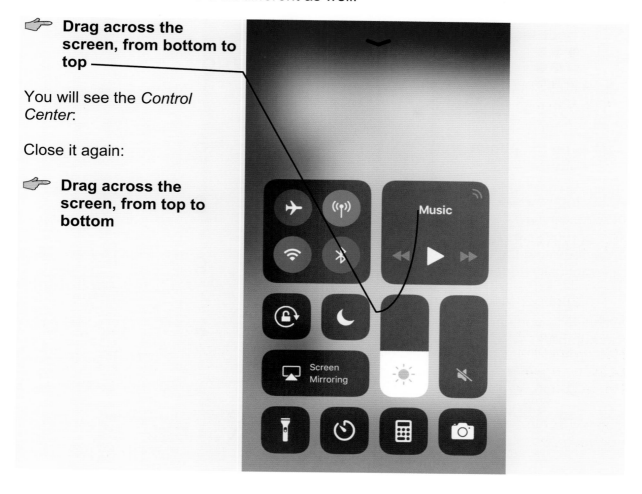

☞ **Drag across the screen, from bottom to top** ——

You will see the *Control Center*.

Close it again:

☞ **Drag across the screen, from top to bottom**

8.2 Making Calls

If you want to make a call, you use the *Phone* app. This app is available on the iPhone, but also if you have an iPad with 3G/4G and have inserted a SIM card in the iPad. This app is not available on the iPad with Wi-Fi.
You open the *Phone* app from the home screen of your iPhone:

At the bottom of the screen:

☞ **Tap**

You dial the phone number of the person you wish to call:

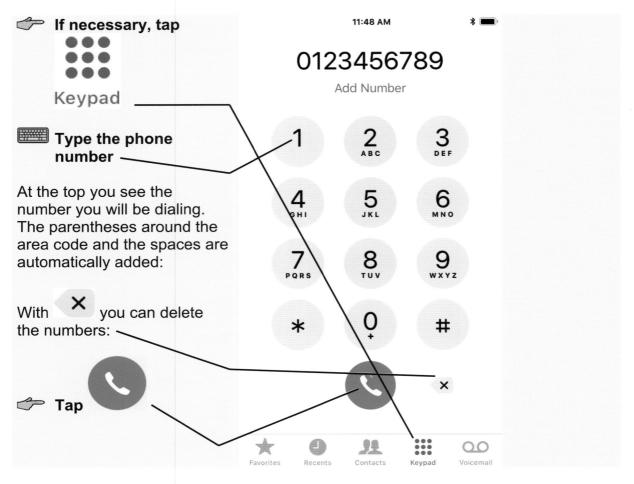

☞ **If necessary, tap**

Keypad

⌨ **Type the phone number**

At the top you see the number you will be dialing. The parentheses around the area code and the spaces are automatically added:

With ✕ you can delete the numbers:

☞ **Tap**

You can hear the telephone ring:

If you want to finish the call, you can briefly press the Sleep/Wake button on the side of your iPhone.

As soon as the person you call picks up, the calling time will be indicated here:

When the conversation is terminated, you can disconnect:

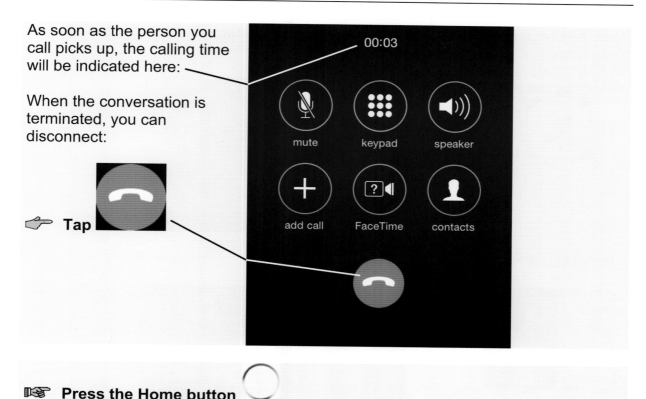

00:03

mute   keypad   speaker

add call   FaceTime   contacts

☞ **Tap**

 Press the Home button

During a call, the screen will turn off when you hold the iPhone to your ear. Once you take the iPhone away from your ear, you will see a number of call options on the screen:

     Puts a conversation on hold.

     Brings the keys in view, so you can choose from a menu.

     Renders the call through a speaker.

     Initiates another phone call (while the other call is on hold).

     Starts a video call with *FaceTime* with the current caller. If a question mark appears on the button, *FaceTime* is not possible with this contact.

    Brings up the list of saved contacts, for example, to look up a phone number during the call.

If you receive a call yourself, you answer the call as follows. If the phone is still in sleep mode:

☞ **Drag the slider**

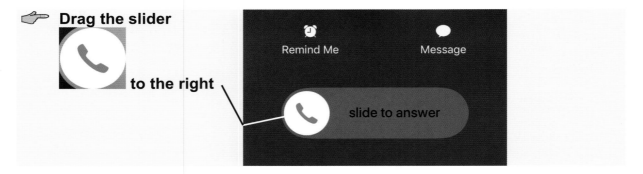

to the right

If the phone is not in sleep mode:

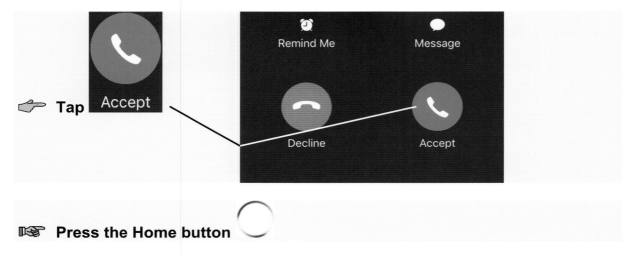

☞ **Tap** Accept

☞ **Press the Home button**

💡 **Tip**
Refusing a call

You can tap the Decline button to send an incoming call straight to your voicemail. This only works if your phone is not in sleep mode when the call comes in.

If your phone is in sleep mode, you can refuse a call as follows:

☞ **Press the Sleep/Wake button twice briefly**

8.3 Making Video Calls with FaceTime

Your iPhone and your iPad too, have their own app for making video calls: *FaceTime*. Although there is a restriction: you can only make calls to other iPhone, iPad, iPod Touch, or Mac users. In order to use *FaceTime* you need to have an Internet connection and an *Apple ID*.

First, you open the *FaceTime* app:

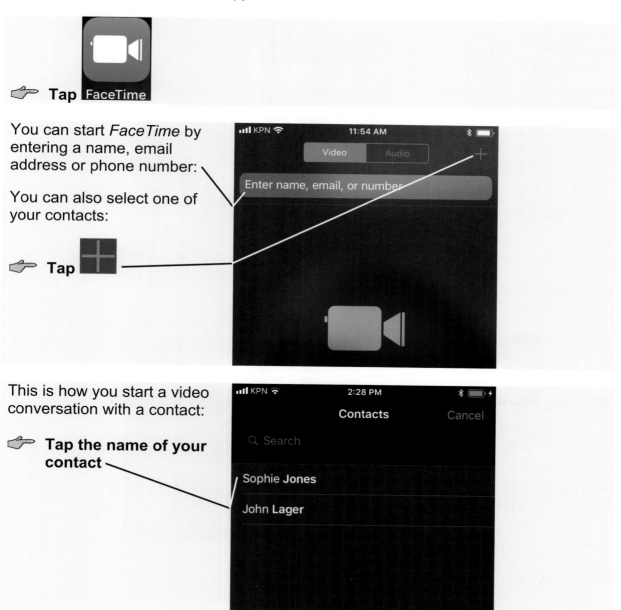

☞ Tap FaceTime

You can start *FaceTime* by entering a name, email address or phone number:

You can also select one of your contacts:

☞ Tap ➕

This is how you start a video conversation with a contact:

☞ **Tap the name of your contact**

For video calling:

☞ **Tap**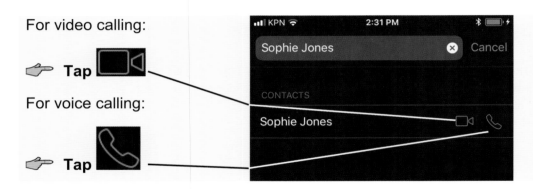

For voice calling:

☞ **Tap**

The device will try to make a connection. You will hear the phone ring. Once the connection has been made, you will be able to see and hear your contact.

In this way you can hold a video conversation with contacts all over the world.

Use the [   ] button to mute the sound of your microphone:

If you want to end the conversation:

☞ **Tap**

With the [↻] button you can use the camera on the back of the iPhone:

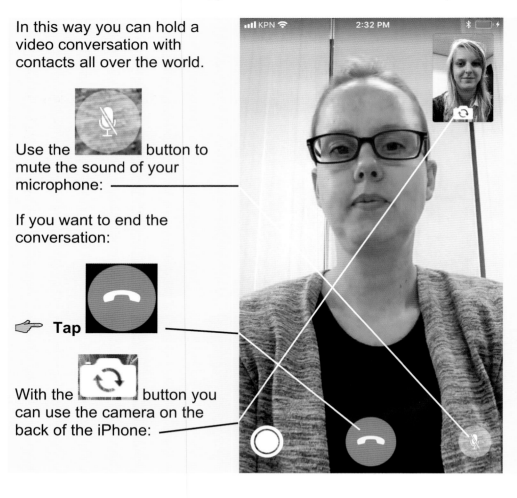

Tip

FaceTime from within the Contacts app

You can also open the *FaceTime* app from within the *Contacts* app. Simply tap the

button that you see by your contact's information.

 Tip

Skype

Another frequently used app for making video calls is *Skype*. You can download this app for free in the *App Store*. The advantage of *Skype* is that you can also communicate with people who do not have an iPhone or iPad, because *Skype* also functions on *Android* tablets and phones, and on computers.

8.4 The Messages App

For sending a message you can use the *Messages* app. On the iPhone, it allows you to send a SMS or *iMessage* message. On the iPad, you can only use the *Messages* app for sending a text message if you have a mobile data plan with SIM card. You do however have the ability to send *iMessages* with your iPad to other users with an *Apple ID*.

☞ **Tap**

You see the *Messages* screen. You are going to send a new email:

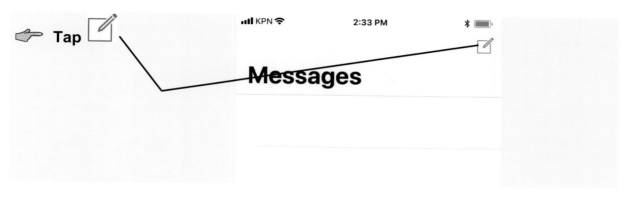

☞ **Tap**

 Type the first letter of the name of your contact

A list of contacts with the same first letter appears:

☞ **Tap the desired contact**

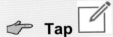 **Tip**

Typing a telephone number or email address of an Apple ID

Instead of selecting a contact, by To: you can also type a phone number. The parentheses are automatically added. You can do the same with an email address. This only works if the receiver uses that email address as their *Apple ID*.

HELP! I see a different page.

If you previously sent or received messages, you will see a list of these messages here. You can then start a new message as follows:

☞ **Tap** 📝

If necessary, you can add any additional recipients:

You do not need to do this now.

At the bottom of the screen:

☞ **Tap** iMessage **or** Text Message

💡 Tip

SMS or iMessage

If you see Text Message, your message will be sent as an SMS and you may be charged a fee from your provider. If you see iMessage, this means the receiver has an iPhone, iPad or iPod Touch, and *iMessage* is activated for both of you. Your message is then sent for free through the Internet, either with the use of a mobile data network (3G/4G) or with Wi-Fi. For 3G/4G you do have to pay the costs of data usage, but that is only about 140 bytes per message. The procedure for sending SMS and *iMessages* is the same.

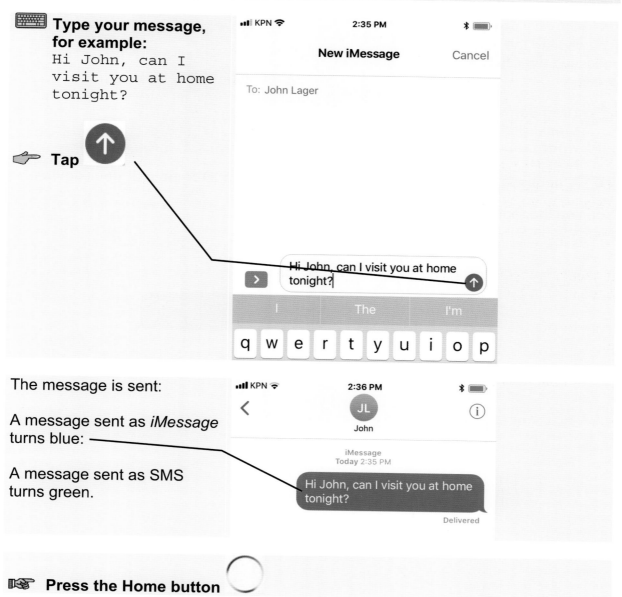

⌨ **Type your message, for example:**

Hi John, can I visit you at home tonight?

☞ **Tap** ⬆

The message is sent:

A message sent as *iMessage* turns blue:

A message sent as SMS turns green.

☞ **Press the Home button**

If you receive an SMS or *iMessage* and the sound of your device is turned on, you will hear a sound signal.

If your device is in sleep mode, the screen lights up and you can read the message: ————

If you do not turn sleep mode off directly, the same will happen two minutes later, as a reminder:

You can tap the received message directly to send a reply:

 Drag across the message from left to right ———

📱 **If necessary, give your passcode or use Touch ID to unlock your device**

You see the reply below your sent message: ——

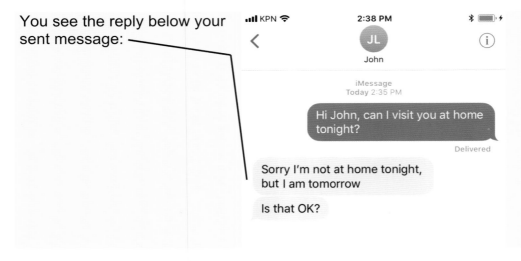

If you wait too long, or were away at the time, the notification will disappear. A new badge will then appear on top of the *Messages* app:

The number 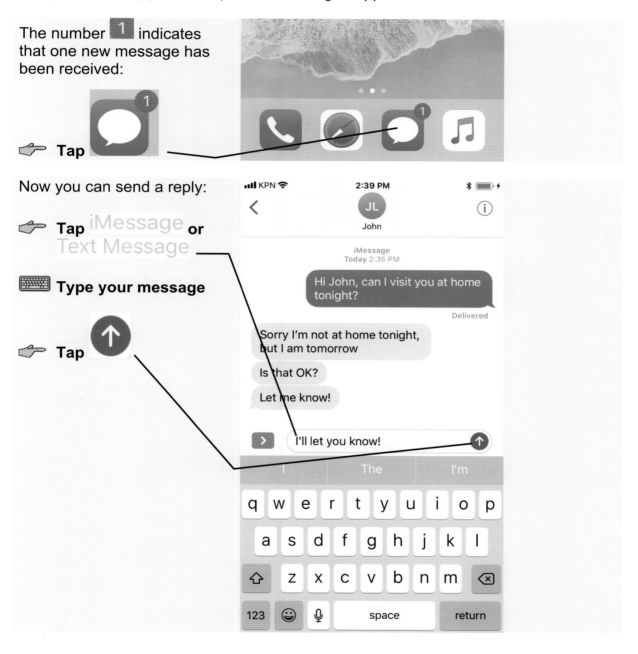 indicates that one new message has been received:

☞ **Tap**

Now you can send a reply:

☞ **Tap** iMessage **or** Text Message

⌨ **Type your message**

☞ **Tap**

You can also delete a message. This may be convenient, for example, if you want to free up some memory space on your iPhone or iPad:

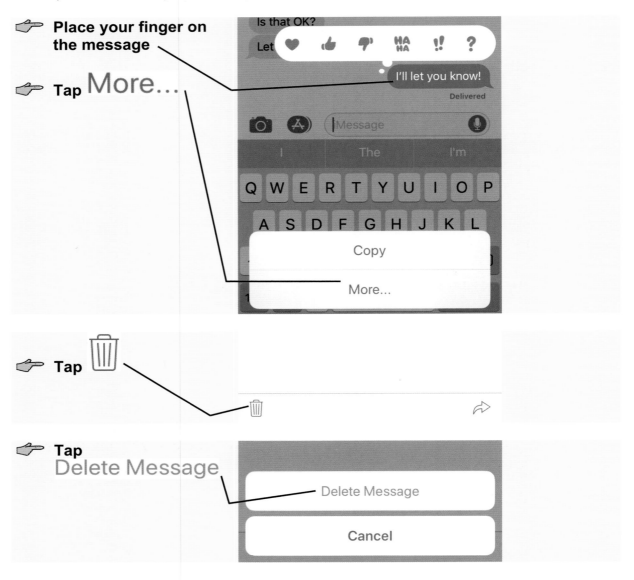

☞ **Place your finger on the message**

☞ **Tap** More...

☞ **Tap** 🗑

☞ **Tap** Delete Message

The message is deleted. You can also delete this person's entire conversation. For this you need to go back to the summary view of all the messages:

☞ **Tap** <

☞ **Tap** Edit

You select the conversation you want to delete:

☞ **Tap the conversation**

At the bottom of the screen:

☞ **Tap** Delete

The entire conversation is deleted.

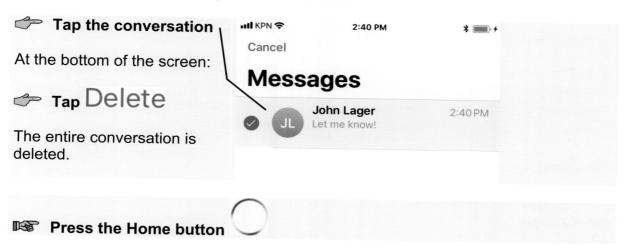

☞ **Press the Home button**

When you send a message to another iPhone, iPad or iPod Touch user, it automatically attempts to send your message with *iMessage*. This message is sent over the Internet, without having to pay for SMS charges. You can view the *iMessage* settings:

☞ **Open the *Settings* app**

☞ **If necessary, swipe upwards over the screen**

☞ **Tap** 💬 Messages

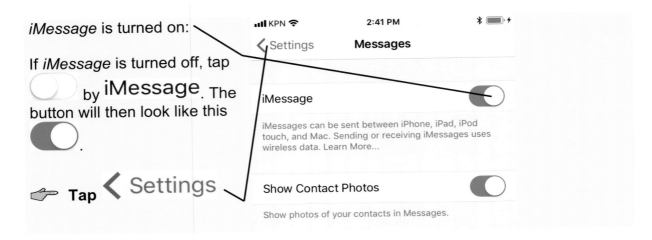

iMessage is turned on:

If *iMessage* is turned off, tap

 by **iMessage**. The button will then look like this

.

Tap ‹ Settings

💡 **Tip**

iMessages on all your Apple devices
If you want to look at your *iMessages* on all your Apple devices, such as an iPad, it is important that you use the same *Apple ID* on all these devices.

If you send a message, and in the text field you see Text Message instead of iMessage , your contact is not using *iMessage*. Your message will then automatically be sent as a SMS. The procedures for sending a SMS or *iMessages* are the same.

🖙 **Press the Home button**

💡 **Tip**

WhatsApp
A very popular alternative to making regular calls and sending text messages is the *WhatsApp* app. This app combines the features of *Skype* and *iMessage*, among other things.
You can use *WhatsApp* for calling, sending text messages, sharing photos and videos, and chatting over the Internet. For example, if you are using Wi-Fi, you can use *WhatsApp* for calling and sending text messages without incurring additional costs. An advantage over *iMessage* is that *WhatsApp* is also available for other operating systems, such as *Android* and *Windows*. This means you can call with users that do not have an iPhone, and send them messages, provided they have installed *WhatsApp*. You can download *WhatsApp* for free in the *App Store*.

8.5 Using Mobile Data

You may also have access to the Internet on your iPhone, through a subscription with a mobile data provider. This means that using the Internet without a Wi-Fi connection will cost you money. For example, when you visit web pages, send *iMessage* messages, or use other apps that have access to the Internet.

It is wise to check what the settings are for using mobile data:

☞ **Open the *Settings* app** 👣**1**

👉 **Tap** 📶 **Cellular**

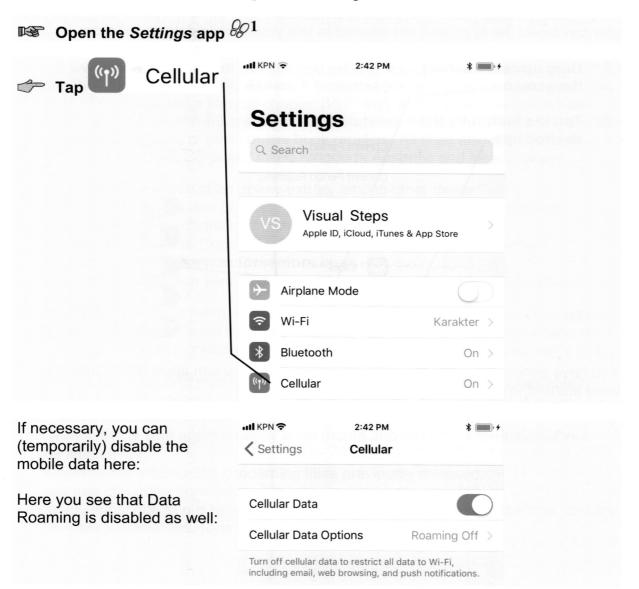

If necessary, you can (temporarily) disable the mobile data here:

Here you see that Data Roaming is disabled as well:

8.7 Background Information

Dictionary

Android	Operating system for cell phones and tablet computers, the counterpart of the *iOS* system made by Apple.
Contacts	The people you have agreed to communicate with.
Data roaming	*Data Roaming* (also called roaming) means that you use the data network of another provider, in case your own provider cannot be reached. If you enable this function in foreign countries this may lead to high costs.
FaceTime	App that lets you make free video calls through the Internet with contacts around the world. The disadvantage of *FaceTime* is that it only allows contact with other iPad, iPhone, iPod touch or Mac users.
iMessage	Feature that lets you send free messages to other iPhone, iPad and iPod Touch users over 3G, 4G or Wi-Fi. When sent over 3G or 4G, data charges may be incurred, but a text message is usually a small file and often no more than 140 bytes.
Messages	App that lets you send an SMS or an *iMessage*.
Mobile data	MBs you use when surfing the Internet through the mobile data network.
Skype	An app that lets you hold free (video) conversations through the Internet, with contacts all over the world. *Skype* is not just used on iPads and iPhones, but also on *Windows* computers and notebooks, and on *Android* and *Windows* smartphones too.
SMS	A text message you can send to others through your cell phone. You will be charged for the costs.
Video call	A conversation with a contact, through a video and sound connection.

Source: iPad User Guide, Skype Help, Wikipedia.

8.8 Tips

 Tip

Raise to wake

iOS contains a feature called *Raise to Wake*. This feature is only available on the latest iPhones. When you lift the device, the screen turns on automatically without having to unlock the iPhone. This lets you get a quick glance at notifications such as incoming email or text messages.

☞ **Tap** Settings , AA **Display & Brightness**

This function is on by default:

To disable this feature:

☞ **By** Raise to Wake,
  tap ⬤◯

The button now looks like this
◯⬤ .

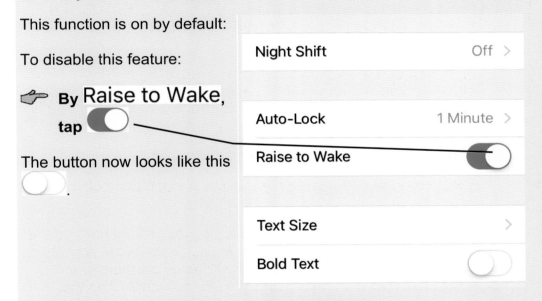

Night Shift	Off >
Auto-Lock	1 Minute >
Raise to Wake	⬤◯
Text Size	>
Bold Text	◯⬤

To turn this feature on again, repeat the same steps.

Notes

Write your notes down here.

Appendix A. How Do I Do That Again?

In this book actions are marked with footsteps: 🐾¹ Find the corresponding number in the appendix below to see how to execute a specific operation.

🐾 **1** **Open *Settings* app**

● Tap Settings

🐾 **2** **Turn on the iPad/iPhone or wake up from sleep mode**

Wake up from sleep mode:

● Press the Home button

Or:

● Press the Sleep/Wake button

Turn on the iPad/iPhone:

● Keep the Sleep/Wake button depressed until you see the *Apple* logo

If you have set up a code:

● Enter the code

If you have set up Touch ID:

● Hold the Home button

🐾 **3** **Select a word**

● Press your finger on the word

● Use the magnifying glass to check if the cursor is positioned on the word

● Release your finger

● Tap Select

🐾 **4** **Open new email message**

● Tap 🖉

🐾 **5** **Open email message**

● If necessary, tap ‹

● Tap the message

🐾 **6** **Add info for contact**

● Tap the desired field, for instance, ➕ add phone

● Type the data

🐾 **7** **Sign in with your *Apple ID***

● Type your password

● Tap OK

Or, if you had signed out:

● Tap Use Existing Apple ID

● Type your email address

● Type your password

● Tap OK

🐾 **8** **Remove app from folder**

● Drag the app out of the folder

🐾 **9** **Send an email**

● Tap To:

● Type the email address

- Tap Subject:
- Type the subject
- If necessary, tap the blank area where you want to type your message
- Type the text
- Tap Send

10 Open *App Store*

- Tap App Store

11 Open *Music* app

- Tap

12 Open *iBooks* app

- Tap iBooks

13 Open *iTunes Store* app

- Tap iTunes Store

14 Scroll to the second page
- Swipe across the screen from right to left

15 Open *Podcast* app

- Tap Podcasts

16 Close a window on a pc
- Click ✕

17 Open *iTunes* on computer

- Double-click iTunes

18 Open *Photos* app

- Tap Photos

19 Open a photo
- If necessary, tap ❮
- Tap the photo

20 Open *Safari* app

- Tap

21 Open a website
- Tap the address bar

- If necessary, tap

- Type the web address

- Tap

22 Open *Files* app

- Tap

23 Open a website on the computer
From the desktop:

- Click

- Type the web address in the address bar

- Press

Appendix B. Installing iTunes and Connecting the iPad to the Computer

In this appendix you can read how to download and install *iTunes*. *iTunes* can be downloaded (for free) from the Apple website, the manufacturers of the iPad and *iTunes*. Next, you open *iTunes* and set up the initial settings for using *iTunes*.

 Please note:

In this book we will install version 12 of the *iTunes* program. But there may be a more recent version of this program, by the time you start using this book. In that case, just look for buttons that resemble the buttons we describe in this appendix.

The first step is to download the *iTunes* program. You will find this program on the Apple website.

👉 **Surf to www.apple.com/itunes/download** 🐾²³

Apple will ask if you want to sign up for product news and special offers. But you do not need to enter your email address to download *iTunes*:

🖱 **Uncheck the boxes** ☑️

👉 **If necessary, select your location** ──

🖱 **Click**
Download now

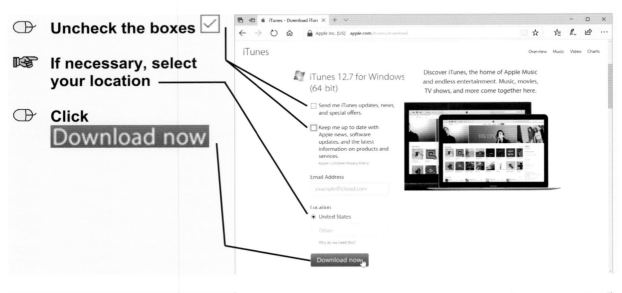

You will see the progress of the download operation:

Run the download file:

⊕ **Click**

In a few moments, you will see the installation window with information about *iTunes*:

⊕ **Click** Next >

In the next window you can select the installation options for *iTunes*:

In this example, a shortcut will be added to the desktop and *iTunes* will be the default player for playing audio files.

You can also change the language, if you want:

⊕ **Click** Install

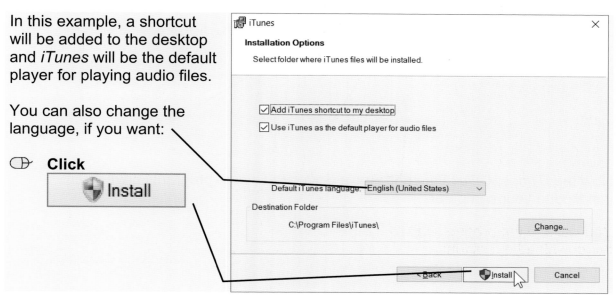

Your screen now turns dark. You will be asked for permission to continue with the installation.

☞ Give permission to continue

Now the *iTunes* program will be installed and if needed, the *QuickTime* program also. *QuickTime* is the multimedia platform from the Apple Corporation; you will need this program if you want to use *iTunes*. This may take several minutes.

The installation process continues:

After the installation has finished, you do not need to open *iTunes* right away:

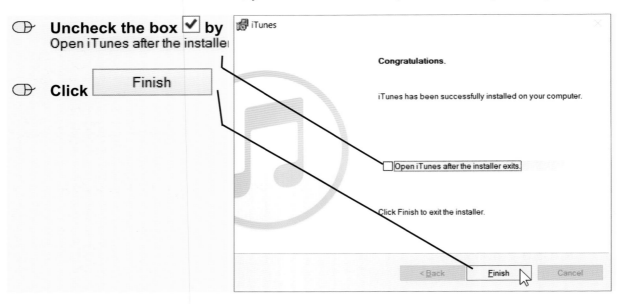

☞ **Uncheck the box** ✔ **by** Open iTunes after the installer

☞ **Click** Finish

Now the *iTunes*, *QuickTime* and *Apple Software Update* programs have been installed to your computer.

☞ Close the browser ௸16

You will start the *iTunes* program on your computer or laptop. On the desktop of your computer a shortcut is placed:

☞ **Double-click**

Most likely you will see a window asking you to accept the software license agreement:

☞ **Click** **Agree**

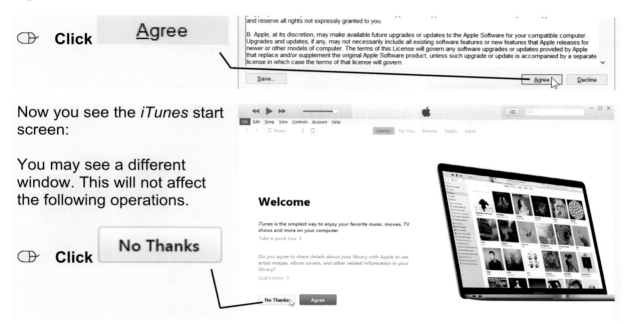

Now you see the *iTunes* start screen:

You may see a different window. This will not affect the following operations.

☞ **Click** **No Thanks**

Now you are going to connect the iPad to your computer. This is how you do it:

👉 **Connect the broad end of the white Lightning-to-USB-cable to the iPad**

👉 **Connect the other end of the cable to one of the USB ports on your computer**

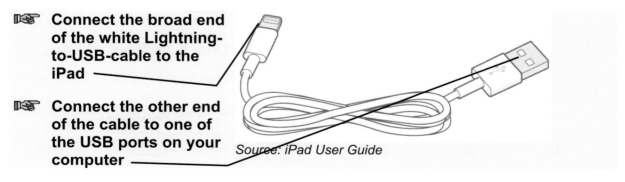

Source: iPad User Guide

If your iPad has a passcode, you may be asked to grant the computer access to the iPad:

⌨ **If necessary, type the passcode on the iPad**

☞ **Drag this slider to the right, to switch off the iPad**

☞ **Once again, keep the Sleep/Wake button depressed until you see the Apple logo appear**

☞ **Download and install (once more) the most recent *iTunes* version from the www.apple.com/itunes/download website**

☞ **Try to re-connect your iPad, preferably to a different USB port**

Assign an easily identifiable name to your iPad:

iTunes suggests giving your iPad the same name as your user account. You can change this:

⎘ **Click the iPad's name**

⌨ **Type a different name, if you wish** ⎯⎯⎯⎯⎯

Although *iTunes* does not automatically synchronize tracks, photos, or other items if you have not started such an operation yourself before, the standard setting is that *iTunes* will still start synchronizing by itself when you connect it to the computer. This happened when you connected the iPad to the pc the first time as well. In that case, no data has been transferred to the iPad, but only a backup copy of the iPad has been created.

During synchronization, at the top of the window a progress bar indicating the progress of the synchronizing operation is shown:

You can continue when you see the Apple logo:

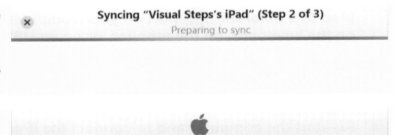

Synchronizing means the content of your iPad will be matched to the content of your *Library*. Tracks, videos, and apps that no longer appear in your *iTunes Library* will be removed from your iPad during synchronization. You will be able to manage the content of your iPad more easily when you disable the automatic synchronization altogether and manually start the synchronization operation whenever you feel like it.

You are going to check the settings for automatic synchronization:

☞ **Click** Edit

☞ **Click** Preferences...

You will see a window with various sections:

☞ **Click** Devices

☞ **If necessary, check the box** ☑ **by** Prevent iPods, iPhones and iPads from syncing automatically

☞ **Click** OK

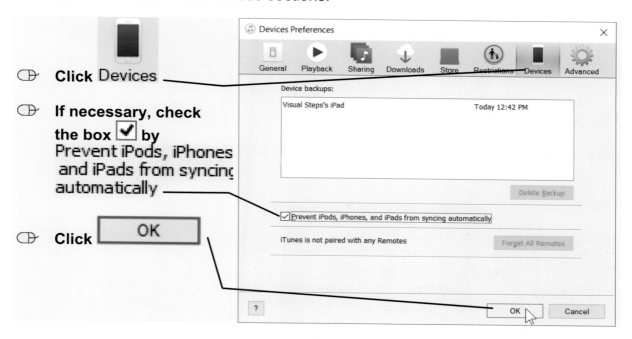

Now you will see the *Summary* tab:

This iPad's software is up-to-date:

In this example a backup copy of the iPad is made on the computer. You can also make and store a backup copy to *iCloud*:

Here you see the available capacity of the iPad:

⊕ **If necessary, drag the scroll bar downwards**

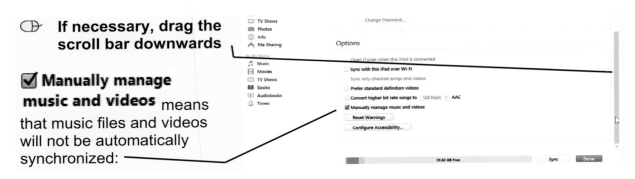

☑ **Manually manage music and videos** means that music files and videos will not be automatically synchronized:

You can disconnect the iPad from your computer any time you want, unless the device is being synchronized with your computer.

If the synchronization is in progress, you will see this message at the top of the *iTunes* window:

When you see this, you can disconnect the iPad:

This is how you disconnect your iPad from *iTunes*:

⊕ **By your iPad's name, click ⏏**

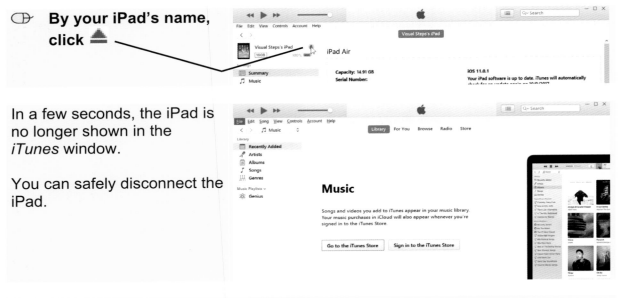

In a few seconds, the iPad is no longer shown in the *iTunes* window.

You can safely disconnect the iPad.

☞ **Disconnect the iPad**

You can now close *iTunes*:

☞ **Close iTunes** ¹⁶

Appendix C. Index

Switch between apps	139, 150
Synchronize	44, 51
iCloud	190
iTunes	248
with another Apple device	34

T

Tablet computer	44
Talk to the iPad	120
Timer	35
Touch ID	21, 25, 41, 44, 199
Touch ID sensor	25
Trash	63, 69
Turn off iPad	40

U

Underline text	61
Unlock iPad	18
Update	
apps	148
iPad	27, 43

V

Video	
copy to computer	170
copy to iPad	173, 183
formats	188
play	168
shoot	161
upload to *YouTube*	170
Video call	223, 236
Videos app	155
Views in *Photos* app	163, 166
Volume	
buttons	25
set	34
VPN	6, 44

W

Web page	80
WhatsApp	232

Widgets	32, 205
Wi-Fi	17, 20, 34, 35, 44
connect with	20, 35
Wireless network (see Wi-Fi)	17

Z

Zoom	81, 92, 160, 165

0

3G/4G-network	17, 27, 38, 44